About the Author

Photo by Bob Blakey

Born in Hamilton, Ontario, in 1955, Cope attended the University of Waterloo, graduating with a B.Sc. in Earth Sciences in 1978. He came to Calgary that same year to work in the oil patch, but his love for writing led him to freelance journalism and a career as a feature writer and business reporter. In 1993, Cope and his wife, Linda, quit their jobs, sold their house, and ran away to the South Pacific. Since then, they have lived in London and Paris and travelled around the world. They currently live in Calgary. ■

Cover design by David Drummond
Cover image by WorldFoto / Alamy
Interior design by Dean Pickup
Edited by Alex Frazer-Harrison
Copyedited by Geri Rowlatt
Proofread by Lesley Reynolds
Maps by Brian Smith / Articulate Eye

The type in this book is set in Sabon.

The publisher gratefully acknowledges the support of The Canada Council for the Arts and the Department of Canadian Heritage.

 Canada Council Conseil des Arts
for the Arts   du Canada

We acknowledge the financial support of the Government of Canada through the Book Publishing Industry Development Program (BPIDP) for our publishing activities.

Printed in Canada by Friesens

06 07 08 09 10 / 5 4 3 2 1

First published in the United States in 2007 by
Fitzhenry & Whiteside
121 Harvard Avenue, Suite 2
Allston, MA 02134

Library and Archives Canada Cataloguing in Publication
Cope, Gordon, 1955-
    So. we sold our house and ran away to the South Pacific / Gordon Cope.

ISBN-13: 978-1-894856-99-7
ISBN-10: 1-894856-99-6

1. Cope, Gordon, 1955- —Travel—Australasia. 2. Cope, Gordon, 1955-
—Travel—Oceania. 3. Australasia—Description and travel. 4. Oceania—
Description and travel. I. Title.

DU23.5.C66 2006   919.04   C2006-902901-6

Fifth House Ltd.
A Fitzhenry & Whiteside Company
1511, 1800-4 St. SW
Calgary, Alberta T2S 2S5

1-800-387-9776
www.fitzhenry.ca

So, We Sold Our House and Ran Away to the

SOUTH PACIFIC

GORDON COPE

FIFTH
HOUSE

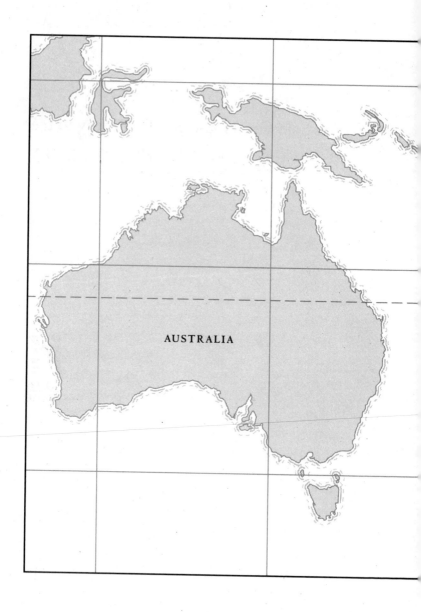

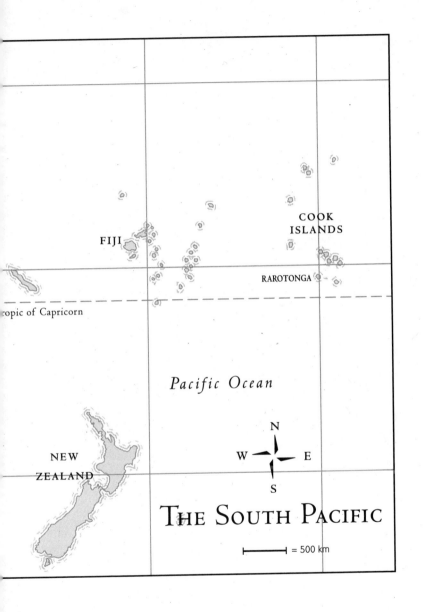

Tropic of Capricorn

FIJI

COOK
ISLANDS

RAROTONGA

Pacific Ocean

NEW
ZEALAND

N
W · E
S

THE SOUTH PACIFIC

= 500 km

We have no more right to consume happiness without producing it than to consume wealth without producing it.

—George Bernard Shaw

*To my wife, Linda, for accompanying me
on the greatest journey of all.*

Note to Readers

I have converted most currency amounts in the book to Canadian-dollar equivalents to spare you the nuisance of having to look up exchange rates. Also, please note that I have made every effort to be as factual and truthful about events in this book as possible, except for the parts I made up. Kindly direct all praise, adulation, and commendations to the author; if you want to whine about something, phone your mother.

—G. Cope

Contents

Prologue: How to Disconnect without Short-circuiting   1

Chapter 1: Barbecuing with Cannibals   11

Chapter 2: Making a Racquet   27

Chapter 3: A Date with Porkchop   45

Chapter 4: Oz You Like It   61

Chapter 5: A Room with a Cockroach   77

Chapter 6: Christmas Down Under   95

Chapter 7: Little Penguins and Skinks   113

Chapter 8: Some Mighty Fine Wine   131

Chapter 9: Auckland Ahoy   149

Chapter 10: The Headless Ghost   165

Chapter 11: Queenstown Beckons   180

Chapter 12: *Palapa* Hammock and Lie Down   198

Epilogue   212

Acknowledgements   214

How to Disconnect without Short-circuiting

It is a warm September evening on the island of Rarotonga. The sun has gone down and a cool, refreshing breeze is blowing in off the Pacific Ocean. My wife, Linda, and I are sitting at a café table anchored into soft, white sand. In the distance, Cook Islanders walk along the barrier reef that has been exposed at low tide. They carry lanterns in one hand and large butterfly nets in the other, ready to catch the flying fish that are attracted to the light. Behind us, beyond the muted bustle of the capital city of Avarua, rise the forest-covered cliffs of the central island.

The owner of the Metua Café arrives with two orders of her house specialty: immense hamburgers that, in addition to the usual burger and bun, contain a fried egg, a slice of sugar beet, and a slice of pineapple, all held together with a bamboo skewer. A gecko on the patio roof chirps approvingly as she places our meal down upon the table, along with two bottles of ice-cold Cooks Lager.

As we dig into our meal, the full moon begins to rise. I've admired the moon countless times—big, orange, harvest disks over Paris, cold orbs above frozen prairies, and hot, burning saucers rising through the smoke of forest fires—but none of those prepares me for the Cook Islands' version. Far across the ocean, somewhere near Peru, it makes its appearance, first, the merest sliver of white, then suddenly, an immense circle of pure silver rising out of the South Pacific. Cold, majestic, and scarred, it casts a glow that lights up the beach so brightly that the fishermen on the reef break off their toils to gaze upon it. The night birds calling from the swaying palms fall silent, and even the clouds that drift low upon the horizon part to let it pass.

Linda and I look at each other and smile. Does it get any better than this?

Some might think that this is a story about the adventures of travel, or maybe beet burgers, but they'd be wrong. It's actually about the pursuit of happiness. Only six months before, we were residing in Calgary, waist deep in March snow and up to our necks in debt. Linda sat at our dining-room table, sorting through a mountain of bills, mostly run up trying to keep Firefly Manor, our dilapidated home in downtown Calgary, from falling down around our ears.

"I don't know how we're going to keep up with all this," she sighed, as the furnace made an ominous belching noise in the basement.

"Maybe you could ask your boss for a promotion," I said. Linda worked as a computer specialist for a large oil company. Surely, they could afford a few more bucks for all the overtime she put in keeping their system limping along.

Linda almost squirted coffee through her nose. "Or you could ask the newspaper for a raise." I laughed ruefully. I worked as a feature writer, covering everything from how to live in a teepee to bobsledding for the blind. My newspaper was so cheap they handed out bus tickets when sending you on assignment.

We were interrupted by Linda's pager. She pulled it off her belt, glanced at the message, then stood up from the table.

"The computer system's frozen up again. I have to go downtown and help fix it."

As she pulled on her winter coat, I noticed her rubbing her side. "Something bothering you?"

"It's that damn vibrating pager. My muscles start to twitch just thinking about it." We both knew it wasn't the pager, though. It was the boring, repetitive nature of the work, unsung and unheralded, that was driving her crazy.

My job only made my brain twitch. Some people view journalism as an exalted profession in which reporters comfort the afflicted and afflict the comfortable. I like to think of it more as a sausage factory, in which endless mounds of glorified gossip are assembled into prose and cranked out for consumption. The most common underlying trait of the newspaper room is heartfelt cynicism, mixed with morbid humour. Over the last six years, I had gone from starry-eyed cub reporter to hard-nosed journalist.

But, I suppose Linda and I were lucky. At least we had jobs.

The following morning when I showed up for my shift, Cranston, the balding assignment editor, handed me a story sheet. "They just laid off fifty workers at the drill-bit factory. Give me fifteen inches."

Ah, now this is what I signed up for—the opportunity to interview recently canned employees on a subject that makes tar look scintillating. "Got anything else?"

Cranston flitted through his pile. "The dead kid that got run over by the ice cleaner—it's the one-year anniversary."

Oh, Lord. Suddenly, drill bits are looking a whole lot better. "What do you want me to do?"

"Interview the parents. See if you can get 'em to sit on a Zamboni. It'll make a nice photo."

Now I knew why all great writers imbibe like tuna. That evening, I joined my friend Brendan at a pub named after James Joyce. Brendan is a scribbler of prose and a part-time accordion musician, known for his love of everything fermentable. After about three pints, Brendan noticed I was not in my usual ebullient mood and tactfully mentioned the fact. "You look like crap. What's wrong with you?"

The truth was, my job was sapping away my love for writing and, without that, what else did I have? "Are you happy with your life?" I asked.

"Who's to say?" Brendan was very metaphysical, especially when drunk. "What *is* happiness?"

That's a good question. Science rather dryly defines happiness as an emotional state caused by dopamine discharging in the brain; anything from shopping for shoes to nibbling someone in a friendly manner can release it. Philosophers aren't much help on the subject, either. Aristotle thought the height of joy was plotting political campaigns. Playwrights and poets don't tend to do a much better job. Shakespeare's Romeo rambles on and on about how delirious the mere sight of Juliet makes him, but the ending isn't exactly a laugh riot. Byron does a good turn about trees and brooks and flowers in his poem to his sister, *Epistle to Augusta*, until he veers into incest and takes a runner to Greece.

It seems, in fact, that it's easier to define happiness by what it's not. "Look at that oilman over there," said Brendan.

"Which one?"

"The one wearing the suit and the fancy Rolex. The one telling the pneumatic blonde all about his ski chalet in BC."

"What about him?"

"Do you think *he's* happy? Of course not, and I'll tell you why." Brendan extended a long, bony finger into the air. "First of all, money can't buy you love."

"I think I heard that somewhere before."

Brendan belched slightly, then continued. "Secondly, happiness comes from doing what you truly enjoy, for no other reason than you love to do it. Finally, happiness is having good friends."

"Here, here." We clinked our glasses.

"Good, I'm glad you agree." Brendan signalled the waitress. "My friend here is buying the next round."

That Friday night, Linda and I were settled in the living room to watch a travel documentary. I went to the kitchen to fetch two glasses of wine and discovered the fridge was warm; the compressor was on the blink.

"Oh, great," said Linda. "We're maxed out on the credit cards. What are we going to do?" A picture of a sun-drenched beach, palm trees swaying in the background, appeared on the TV. She snuggled up against me on the couch. "Why don't we just quit our jobs, sell the house, and run away to the South Pacific?"

"Yeah, sure. You can knit macramé owls and I'll sell strawberry crepes on the beach." I turned off the TV and we went to bed.

I tried to sleep, but couldn't get Linda's idea out of my head. Why *not* dump it all and run away to the South Pacific? It's got warm weather and miles and miles of sandy shores, and it doesn't have snow shovels. You've got to love a place like that. But quitting your job and selling your house is just silly. Everybody fantasizes about it, but nobody *does* it. So, why was I even considering it? If it was just a mid-life crisis, I could buy a new sports car or take a bubble bath. But it was something more than that—both Linda and I were deeply unhappy. Is that sufficient reason to run away? Do we *deserve* happiness?

Several days later, I was sitting in the paper's cafeteria with Stuart, the business columnist. Stuart, who was in his fifties, wore a wrinkly suit and a scowl nurtured by twenty-five years in the newspaper business. Having just given up smoking, he was well on his way to breaking the world's record for coffee consumption. By 10 o'clock that morning, he was, by my count, on his seventeenth mug. "I'm thinking of buying a new percolator for my house," he said, pointing to an advertising flyer on the table. "The Bay has one that makes 120 cups."

"That's nice. We were thinking of quitting our jobs, selling our house, and running away to the South Pacific."

Stuart shrugged. "Running away never solved anyone's problems."

"Oh, yeah? How about Gauguin? He split from his life in Paris and became famous painting topless Polynesian babes. And look at Marlon Brando. He bought an island retreat in Tahiti."

"Gauguin died penniless, and Brando turned into the *Goodyear Blimp*." Stuart fell silent and gazed off into the distance. Suddenly, for a brief second, I could see a glimmer of him as a much younger man, back when he still had dreams. "When are you thinking of going?"

"Maybe this fall."

Stuart tilted his head in the direction of the newsroom upstairs. "Are you coming back?"

"Nope."

His scowl softened for the briefest moment. "Good. Because if you did, I'd have to kill you."

In jest, I related my conversation to Linda that evening. "I've been thinking about it, too," she replied. "I mean running away, not killing you."

"Really? Look at everything we'd have to give up."

"Like, what? We hate our jobs and the house is driving us into bankruptcy."

"I know, but it would be such a risk."

"Sure it would." Linda gave me a big hug. "But think of what we have to gain. And we'd be doing it together."

I smiled. "Let's do it."

Once we had crossed the proverbial Rubicon, our decision took on a life of its own. First, we had to decide where to go. The South Pacific is a big place, and we wanted to pick destinations that were accessible and relatively affordable—we didn't want to blow all our money the first few weeks out. Second, the thought of going on a tour package and dashing madly from place to place was out of the question. We needed a chance to check places out thoroughly. I didn't want to discover too late that the paradise we had chosen to flee to had fleas. Finally, we needed a budget and a timetable.

Selling our house would give us enough money to live for a year without working. By happy coincidence, Air New Zealand offered a one-year excursion fare to four sun-drenched destinations that we had always dreamed of visiting. Our first stop would be the Cook Islands; after that, we would move on to Australia, New Zealand, and finally Fiji. We would budget our funds to stay on the road for twelve months. But we also agreed that if we found our paradise sooner, we would put down roots and stay forever.

Our course of action set, we soon discovered that disconnecting from it all without short-circuiting required some effort. Oddly, resigning from the newspaper didn't.

"Good riddance," said the chief assistant editor. "And don't come back."

Selling the house was also easy. "I can get you twice what you paid for it," said the realtor, when I brought him in to appraise it.

My chest puffed out in pride. "Because of all the work I did renovating it?"

"No, because of the lot. I could get *three* times what you paid for it if this old dump wasn't sitting on it."

As for our furniture, what we couldn't sell at a garage sale, we gave to the Sally Ann. The few belongings we wished to keep fit into no more than half a dozen boxes. Strange, isn't it, how few possessions are really important when tropical shores beckon.

Our friends were very sympathetic. "You'll get robbed and pillaged by pirates," said Marjorie, a pal who had known Linda since grade school. "Have fun, though."

Curiously, those with small children seemed to be most supportive. We dropped in for coffee with our soon-to-be-ex-neighbours Fred and Jennifer. Fred, Jr., aged three, was busy tormenting the cat, while one-year-old Elisa was experimenting with projectile Pablum. Jennifer, patiently scraping the purée out of her hair and reloading Elisa, listened intently as we outlined our plans. "Any chance you have spare room in your suitcase? I'd like you to take something along."

"What?"

"Me."

More difficult was telling loving relatives. "What are you going to be, a surf bum?" asked my mother-in-law.

In fact, I had a plan. For years, I'd been turning over an idea for a historical thriller in my head, but had never found the time to create it—now would be the perfect opportunity. "No, I'm going to write a novel."

"Like I said, a bum."

The most difficult part was to have faith in our decision. What if we didn't find happiness? What if we risked our futures and discovered that happiness doesn't really exist? Fortunately, Brendan offered comforting words as we were getting onto the airplane. "Whenever you feel yourself wavering, just think of all your friends back home."

"You mean, about how much love they feel for us?"

"No, how much they envy you. Jealousy is a much-under-rated vice." ■

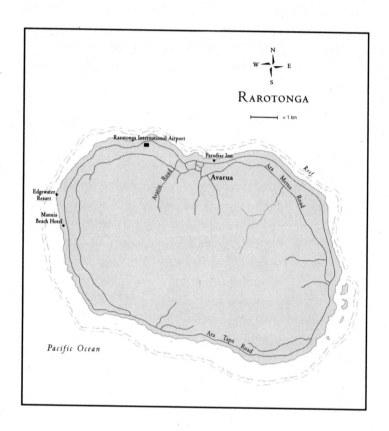

RAROTONGA

= 1 km

Rarotonga International Airport

Paradise Inn

Avarua

Ara Metua Road

Avatiu Road

Reef

Edgewater Resort

Manuia Beach Hotel

Ara Tapu Road

Pacific Ocean

CHAPTER 1

Barbecuing with Cannibals

We arrive in Avarua, Rarotonga, the capital of the Cook Islands, just before dawn on the last Saturday in August. Raro, as it is known locally, sits like an uncut emerald in the middle of the Pacific Ocean, some four thousand kilometres south of the equator. Like the Hawaiian Islands, it is volcanic in origin, with steep, basaltic cliffs thrusting out of turquoise waters. And, like the Hawaiian Islands, it is blessed with a comfortably benign climate year-round, broken only by the occasional cyclone. But that is where all similarity ends. Whereas the city of Honolulu is a large, modern metropolis, the Cook Islands' sleepy capital of Avarua boasts perhaps two thousand souls, including several hundred chickens. Shaped like a potato, the entire island is only about twelve kilometres long and six kilometres wide.

We disembark from the international airport terminal and make our way to the taxi stand. The stand is occupied by some of the country's most ambitious citizens, their primary distinction being that they are awake before everyone else on the island. Tony, the Edgewater Resort's taxi driver, is unrepentantly cheerful as he herds our travel-weary carcasses into his van.

"Welcome, welcome," he greets us, offering the warm smile that is the trademark of all Cook Islanders. "I will take you to the hotel, shortly."

Although we don't realize it at the time, this is our first introduction to the Cook Islands' most famous invention, "Maori Time," which appears to be an adaptation of Einstein's theory of relativity. In the Islands' version, time slows not so much as you approach the speed of light, but as you increase the amount of suntan lotion. Ergo, the nicer the day, the later anything gets done. On truly fine days, time has been known to stand still.

We take our driver's disappearance as a welcome opportunity to recover from the flight, a twelve-hour incarceration with screaming babies and gaseous grandfathers, which left us bleary-eyed and breathless. As we stretch our legs and gaze upon the morning light illuminating the nearby cliffs, we suck in the warm, moist air, admire the bird-of-paradise flowers growing wild beside the airport tarmac, and thank our lucky stars we've finally arrived.

It's a premature blessing. As our brief sojourn at the taxi stand turns into a half-hour wait, we quickly begin to lose any equanimity engendered by the tropical setting. I approach another cabbie standing nearby, a young man in his mid-twenties, wearing a blue floral-print shirt with the name "PawPaw" written on it. "Excuse me, can you tell me what happened to Tony?"

"He had to go to work," says PawPaw.

"He *was* at work. He was supposed to drive us to the hotel."

Pawpaw breaks into a radiant smile. "No, he only does that at night. In the day, he drives the ambulance." He turns and points to the rising sun. "It is now day."

We drag our luggage out of the abandoned taxi and reload it into Pawpaw's. After a round of handshakes with his fellow cabbies, Pawpaw hops into the driver's side and soon has us on the doorstep of the Edgewater Resort. The hotel consists of several wings of walk-up rooms that radiate out from the reception area, all within easy staggering distance of the beach and the frond-covered bar. Our room, priced at $150 per night, is on the third floor of the only wing devoid of an elevator. We gamely lug our bags up the stairwell, all the while surrounded by a less-than-floral odour.

"What did you eat on the plane—dead dog?" asks Linda.

The room turns out to be a large efficiency unit, complete with hot plate, kitchen, and three-piece bath. We drop our luggage on the floor and flop into the comfortably firm, queen-sized bed; within seconds, we are absolutely, blissfully unconscious.

I awake several hours later, refreshed but still somewhat disoriented. I cross the room and open the curtains on the large west-facing window to be greeted by a magnificent view of the Pacific Ocean. The sun burns down brightly upon placid blue water that stretches to the curved horizon. Palm trees frame the pool, the bar, and a large refuse bin, coyly camouflaged by coconut-wood logs. Linda is still fast asleep, so I don a pair of shorts and sneakers and walk down to the carefully groomed beach.

The entire island is encircled by a living coral reef. At the Edgewater Resort, it comes to within about fifty metres of the shore, but it is low tide, and the water has receded out to its edge. I wander out, picking my way between inlets of shallow water. The first thing I note is a loud, clicking sound coming from the cracks within the coral.

"Crabs," explains a young boy, walking barefoot along the reef edge. He pulls several large specimens from a white plastic pail. "My mom boils them for supper."

The boy is about eight or nine and carries a short, wooden stick that he uses to poke into the tidal pools. He has the happy, carefree nature of children the world over, that mixture of joy and curiosity about everything around him. I ask about the creatures in the tide pools and listen intently as he points out tiny blue starfish, slowly clambering their way across bits of coral, and sea cucumbers, which resemble large sausages that have been left to soak in water for a week, slumbering beneath clefts in the rock. He tells me the cucumbers are considered an island delicacy, but judging from their proliferation, it is a delicacy that is infrequently treasured.

The tide begins to turn around suppertime, and the boy departs for home and I return to our room. By then, Linda is awake, and the smells emanating from the restaurant area are very tempting. The Edgewater's restaurant is situated under a *palapa*, a large, open-sided structure, roofed with thatched palm leaves. "You are in luck," our hostess informs us when we arrive. "Tonight is our Famous Island Night."

Famous Island Night includes a rather large buffet and a floor show. The buffet is amply stocked with pork roast baked in pineapple glaze, fish marinated in coconut cream, a starchy tuber called taro root, and deep-fried breadfruit. The dessert, we are disappointed to see, is canned fruit, which is a bit like dishing up biblical comic books in a monastery. We settle in at our table, with umbrella-topped cocktails made of pineapple liqueur and orange juice, to watch the floor show.

The entertainment consists of men and women dressed in local costume and singing traditional songs. The women wear coconut halves tied over their breasts and grass skirts that shimmy and undulate in a most inviting manner—a little too inviting, as a group tour from Australia begins waving their Foster beer cans in the air and shouting lewd suggestions. The drummer, a large, bare-chested warrior, wearing a brightly coloured sarong, diplomatically deals with the intrusion by leaping to his feet, screaming in a most blood-curdling fashion, and rushing the table with his battle spear. This causes a general retreat by the unarmed Aussies, much to the amusement of the rest of the crowd.

We take that as our cue to depart before the show reaches the re-enactment of the first meeting between missionaries and cannibals. We wander back through the grounds, admiring the beautiful starlit sky and the waft of ocean breeze, until we once again come within range of our room.

Linda wrinkles her nose. "Haven't you gotten over that airline food *yet*?" It isn't until we spot a backhoe parked near our unit that we realize all is not well in paradise. We approach cautiously, noses tweaked, and confirm that some sort of large concrete container is being unearthed.

"Looks like a septic tank," I offer. "Make that a *leaky* septic tank."

We retreat to our room, but the ripe odour follows us in. I open the patio doors to let in the ocean breeze, but the band back at Famous Island Night has by now swung into a reggae version of "Que Sera, Sera," and the cacophony is enough to rattle the fillings from my teeth.

"This is awful," says Linda. "We have to get out of here."

I couldn't agree more. Fortunately, we have brought along a guidebook that shows the location of all the motels and hotels on the island. The prices listed for most of them are well below the $150 rate we are paying at the Edgewater. With the help of a moped, the guidebook assures us, we can make an easy tour of the road circling Rarotonga, an ideal way to find accommodation more amenable, and less abusive, to the pocketbook.

After a fitful night of alternating between eau-de-toilet and Doris Day meets Bob Marley, we arise the next morning, determined to find alternate lodgings. A gas station near the resort offers to rent us a scooter for fifteen dollars a day. This is a bargain, the mechanic informs us, as the normal rate is twenty-five dollars, plus mileage.

"Don't let the looks worry you," he reassures us, stubbing out his cigarette with a bare foot, then energetically kicking the small motorcycle to life. "You can pass a Mercedes with this baby."

I silently wonder if Mercedes ever made a tractor. Donning sunglasses and tight-fitting caps, we set off in search of the perfect lodgings.

True to the mechanic's word, and much to my surprise, our scooter actually has some pep. We sail along the main road past huge cedar trees, brightly painted buses, decrepit old lorries stacked with hay, and ample women perched sidesaddle on moped pillion seats, their straw hats fluttering in the wind as their husbands drive them to market. Linda and I sing "Born to be Mild" and wave to everyone as we zip past.

Flying along on a scooter is very different from being chauffeured in a hermetically sealed tour bus. You become part of the environment—not just figuratively, but literally, with tiny bugs sticking to your teeth—but that doesn't stop us from enjoying the countryside. Plots of land in Raro are neatly laid out along the roadway: here a horse pasture, there a taro patch, each separated by a little dirt road, exposing the rich, red volcanic soil beneath. Every few kilometres, a local village appears on the road verge, marked by a petrol station, complete with hand-cranked pumps, and invariably accompanied by a local grocery, distinguished by tin signs advertising ice cream and canned fish. We also pass many family cemeteries, the cement crypts festooned with garlands of jasmine flowers and small, white-painted, wooden crosses, a nod to both contemporary Christian and ancient beliefs.

Several kilometres south of the Edgewater, we come to the Manuia Beach Motel, our first stop. We park our transportation, by now christened Easy Rider, and inspect the premises like seasoned, world-class travellers. The motel is a well-maintained lodge, with thatched-roof huts overlooking a peaceful lagoon. Out near the breakers, fishermen in their boats pole along like gondoliers, and on the horizon, white, fluffy clouds march majestically south. Linda and I don't have to say anything to each other—the place is gorgeous.

I approach the young clerk at the reception desk. "This is a lovely motel," I say. "How much do you charge to stay?"

"Three hundred dollars."

"What, for the week?"

"No, for the night."

I gape like a hick from the sticks. The clerk's asking price is at least double the amount listed in the guidebook, and we hastily leave before we are charged for breathing the air. We continue to drive counter-clockwise around the island, stopping at numerous hotels, but our journey confirms our worst suspicions: all of the lodgings feature rates that are almost as ludicrous as the Manuia's. We finally stop to have lunch on the beach and take stock of our grim situation.

"They want more than we paid to stay in downtown San Francisco," laments Linda. "How could the guidebook be so wrong?"

I sombrely chew my sandwich. Hotel prices had inflated dramatically, and I have no idea why, but suddenly, foul septic tanks, noisy bar bands, and drunken Aussies didn't seem so bad. We finish our meal in silence and continue our journey back to the Edgewater. We just reach the edge of Avarua when Easy Rider begins to cough and sputter. I angle the scooter to the shoulder, where it gives one last spurt, then dies. I spend several minutes kicking the starter, but our ancient cycle refuses to co-operate. Finally, I heave it up onto its stand.

"Maybe it's out of gas," offers Linda.

I shake the bike, and the tank swishes. "No, it sounds like it's still half full. Besides, we've only gone twenty-five kilometres. It can't possibly be out of fuel."

We decide to call the mechanic and have him come pick us up. I look around for a phone and spot a woman, perhaps forty years of age, with blonde hair, a dolphin tattoo on her right ankle, and a green sarong, coming our way. She glances at the scooter, then introduces herself as Karen.

"You having a problem?" she asks.

"It won't start," I explain, lamely. "We rented it from a station near the Edgewater."

Karen shakes her head. "I'm surprised you got this far. Come on, I'll call and have them pick you up."

We walk along the edge of the road, me pushing the bike, until we come to a small hotel. It turns out that Karen is a former nurse from Vancouver, who, several years ago on a week-long holiday to Raro, met Charlie, the son of a local chieftain. Fed up with Vancouver's cold and rain, she eventually decided to give up her calling, move to the Cook Islands, and become the manager of the Paradise Inn. She's been here about two years now, and her North American gait has been replaced by the languid, flip-flop pace of island life.

The hotel, an old, converted dance hall painted a bright pastel peach, has a riot of red bougainvillea clambering up trellises and spilling across the arbours that cover the side verandas. While Karen chews out the mechanic on the phone, Linda and I inspect the hotel. A dozen or so spacious rooms open out through double doors onto a veranda that extends all the way down the building. The back of the lodge features a large, teakwood bar and a patio overlooking the Pacific Ocean. I nudge Linda. "Have a look in the guidebook. How much does it say a room costs?"

Linda thumbs through the accommodation section. "Sixty dollars a night. That means it must be about two hundred dollars by now."

Karen finishes on the phone and hangs up. "He'll be around in about twenty minutes to pick you up. Whatever you do, don't pay him a cent to take you back."

"Thank you for helping us," I reply. "Tell me, what do you charge for your rooms?"

"Sixty dollars a night."

"What? That's what the book says."

"That's what I charge."

"But everyone else on the island is charging at least double."

"I know. They all got together last winter and jacked up the rates."

"Why?"

Karen points toward the Pacific Ocean. "Where else you going to go?" She lights a cigarette and adjusts her sarong. "I told them, you're aiming to shoot yourself in the foot. If you want to keep people coming back, you have to charge what it's worth, not what you can squeeze out of them."

I look at Linda, then back at Karen. "Do you have a room for the next month?"

Karen smiles. "Number 7, on your right."

By supper that evening, the Edgewater is forgotten and we are firmly ensconced on the Paradise Inn patio, gazing out over the Pacific

Ocean. A pair of steaks sizzles enticingly on the hotel's barbecue grill, their marinade sauce wafting in the evening breeze. As the sun dips below the horizon, silhouetting the surrounding palm trees in silky black, we toast one another with a glass of chilled Kiwi Sauvignon Blanc and listen to the symphony of surf crashing against reef.

We have found our little corner of paradise.

For the next few weeks, our life in Raro revolves around anything within walking distance of the Paradise Inn. Unlike holidayers trying to cram every minute full of waterskiing, authentic sausage buffets, and souvenir shopping, our priority is to do as little as humanly possible. For Linda, that involves arising at a suitably late hour every morning, helping herself to a cup of freshly brewed coffee in the bar, and then pulling a lounge chair to the edge of the patio and immersing herself in a Jackie Collins novel.

I, however, am too fidgety for such inert luxury. Too many years in the newspaper business chasing stories for the evening deadline has left me with a regrettable surfeit of energy, and after an hour or so of doing a crossword puzzle, I am invariably seized by the desire to leap up and explore. Linda, understanding my weakness, charitably waves me off. "Just don't do anything foolish, like buying a sailboat," she warns. I wander off in search of adventure and thrills, or at least a decent newspaper.

In my personal travels around the world, I have roamed by train across Malaysia, by hovercraft through Greece, and by bus across Yugoslavia, but I have discovered that, by far, the most enjoyable method of travel is by foot. By this, I don't mean hiking the Himalayas with everything but the kitchen sink strapped to my back; rather, I prefer a destination that is compact and interesting enough to encourage pedestrian exploration. There is nothing more pleasurable than spending the day walking the bustling streets of London, for instance, poking in haberdasheries, trolling for discount theatre tickets at the numerous agencies, and smelling the curries endlessly emanating from corner shops. For the traveller wandering the byways at a leisurely, unstructured pace, the world is a tasty oyster, indeed.

Avarua stretches some three kilometres along Rarotonga's north coast, encompassing the harbour, the House of Parliament, the main shopping district, several ancient churches, and the airport. The harbour draws me like a cigarette butt to a beer bottle. The Cook Islands export bananas, papaya, and coconuts, but most of the activity is imports—everything from cement and building materials to shoes and crème de menthe. In addition to several rusty freighters disgorging cargo, the dock area is filled with yachts from around the world. Most bear the flags of New Zealand or Australia, reflecting the proximity of these countries, but American, Canadian, and even an Irish flag also fly from the stern poles.

It is the Irish boat, an eighteen-metre, teak yacht named the *Rover*, that catches my attention. As I inspect it from the dock, two men disembark in a rubber dinghy and head my way. "Do us a favour and tie the line," shouts the rower to me, as he reaches the dock. I secure the line and help the men ashore. The rower is an Irishman of sixty, his face ruddy from the tropical sun. His mate is an American with a military crewcut, perhaps ten years younger.

"Thank you, lad," says the Irishman. "My name's Captain Billy, and this here's Colonel Mike. Care to join us for a grog?"

It being just after noon, I agree that this is an excellent idea and accompany the two men to the Banana Bar, the Cook Islands' principal watering hole. It is a low, tin-roofed complex of buildings modelled after a missionary's station, albeit one that favours beer over anointed water, in which the teak-panelled rooms are dark and well ventilated and the Cooks Lager draft is chilled to perfection. We find a comfortable table and I soon learn their stories.

Colonel Mike is a former U.S. Army officer who served for thirty years in military intelligence, with all the distinction that occupation implies. Tall, grey-haired, and possessing the retiring nature for which Americans are famous, Colonel Mike has decided to settle on Raro to enjoy its tranquil life, though not necessarily contribute to it.

Immediately upon landing in Raro the week before, Mike hooked up with Captain Billy of Belfast. Billy is an overweight Protestant, who loves to brag about his yacht. For the last six years, he has been sailing the Seven Seas to avoid paying alimony.

"We're looking for a little action," explains Captain Billy, with a wink. "Know any lively girls?"

I doubt if Captain Billy's definition of lively includes choir practice. After several more quarts of lager and a plate of fried bananas, I leave the bar and stagger back toward the Paradise Inn. The kilometre-long walk serves to clear my head somewhat, and by the time I reach my neighbourhood, I am starting to think of supper. A grocery store sits next door to the inn. It's run by Papa Manu, a short, bald butcher who favours his profession's universal uniform, a bloody white apron. In the few days that we have lived at the Paradise Inn, I've noticed the impressive amount of garbage accumulated on Papa Manu's property. Outboard-motor carcasses, washtubs, and piebald tires are to be expected, of course, but he has augmented this with bamboo scaffolding, oil drums, basaltic boulders, and ice cream carts to create a veritable playground of Eden for his herd of children and scrawny chickens.

Today, I notice a large pillar of smoke rising into the palm trees on his property. It is too large for a cookout, unless, of course, the chef is reverting to traditional cuisine. I go into the grocery store and introduce myself as a new neighbour and ask what the fire is about. Papa Manu beams at me from behind the meat counter. "I'm cleaning up the yard—my son turns twenty-one today."

That's as good an excuse as any, I reckon. "Congratulations. Are you planning a party for him?"

"Come with me, you will see."

Journeying through the back door, we pick our way across a muddy patch to the backyard. The oil drums and old washtubs have been shoved onto his neighbour's property, and a large bonfire of coconut husks and shipping palettes accounts for the rest of the missing mess. Several pits have been dug in the soft sand and lined with rocks, and a large tent has been erected over one corner, with several buffet tables set up under it in the shade. Five piglets are tied to the palm trees adjacent to the lagoon, where they munch on corncobs.

Papa Manu leads me to the pigs. "See how fat they are? They will be delicious. It will be a bloody great party, you will see. You must join us."

"Thank you," I reply. I admire the pigs, who, in turn, nervously eye a large oil drum, filled with simmering water. "I'm sure it'll be a wonderful celebration."

We part company, and I scoot through a bamboo patch and back to the inn, where I find Linda in our room. "We've been invited to a party tonight!"

Linda is bent over the hot plate, fiddling with the controls. "Does it include supper?"

"Fresh roast pig."

"Great. I can't figure out how to make this cooker work."

Our room is a delightful contradiction of comfort and idiosyncrasy. Artfully designed to take advantage of the high ceiling and roof vents—a legacy of the dance hall—the sleeping loft is near the overhead fan to ensure cool breezes during the night. The toilet is housed in a little closet, and the shower area is large enough to allow two to bathe. A compact kitchenette area, with fridge, sink, and countertop, leaves sufficient room for a small dinner table and sofa.

Some of our room features are unpredictably annoying, however. The huge palm trees that grow adjacent to the veranda supply much-needed shade during the day, but their fronds noisily drag across the corrugated roof during windy nights, and once, a coconut landed on the tin roof at 3:00 AM, with the impact of a mortar shell. The portable tape deck that serves as our entertainment centre only plays tapes backward, which is just slightly worse than the daily polka hour on the official government FM radio station. Still, our lodging's shortcomings are more than compensated by its charm. The planet already has more cookie-cutter Holiday Inns than it will ever need, and I will gladly trade all the paper toilet sanitizers in the world for the gecko that eats the bugs in our room.

Our supper plans settled, I retire to the patio, there to admire the Pacific Ocean. For those people fortunate enough to live by the ocean, I suppose it is no big thrill. The water is often too cold to swim in, storms erupt without warning, and cool mornings are tinged with a dampness that cuts to the bones. But for those who spend their lives parked in the middle of a continent, it is a balm, indeed. For us, there is nothing so relaxing as sitting by a beach and listening to the surf wash endlessly on the shore.

I no sooner sit down than I spot a spray of mist emanating from the ocean about a hundred metres past the coral reef. I grab the hotel binoculars and focus on the region, hoping to spot a dolphin. To my amazement, the waves part and a whale the size of a bus hurtles forth, splashing down to one side.

I quickly shout for Linda. Karen, hearing the commotion, emerges from her quarters. "Looks like a humpback," she explains, shading her eyes. "She's got a baby, too."

The whales, once nearly extinct, have regained their former numbers and are now seen quite frequently around the Cook Islands. They spend most of the summer months feeding off Antarctica, but when the cooler weather creates ice cover, they journey north to the equator, where they mate or give birth. In September, they begin their long journey southward again, travelling in small packs with their young.

Karen is right; the first small plume I saw belonged to a baby whale. We can clearly discern two pointed humps, periodically breaking the water as they troll adjacent to the reef. At one point, the five-metre-long offspring breaks the surface half a dozen times in a row. "Nobody knows why they do it," says Karen. "There's no biological or feeding reason. Maybe they're just happy nobody's trying to kill them any more."

We are interrupted in our musings by a blood-curdling scream from next door—Papa Manu is dispatching the first of the pigs. Amid much squealing and agony, the main course is drained and gutted in an old bathtub and shorn of its bristles in the coals of the fire, before being dunked in the oil drum of simmering water to cleanse and soften its exterior. The carcass is then wrapped in banana leaves and wet cardboard and buried in a barbecue pit. Linda and I cringe at the spectacle, but Karen merely shrugs.

"How can you stand it?" I ask.

"Ever wonder how they get your breakfast bacon into those tidy little packets?"

An elderly couple, dressed in matching khaki shorts, canvas bush hats, and Adidas walking shoes, appears on the hotel patio. The woman, who is wearing a pair of reading glasses on a chain around her neck, places the eyewear on the bridge of her nose and reads the rates posted behind the reception desk. She finally speaks, in a heavy German accent. "You haf lodgings available, *ja*?"

"You've got a choice between which side you want a room on," offers Karen. "You can stay on the east side, which features roosters, or you can go with the special events on the west side." She cocks a thumb over her shoulder as another one of the porkers meets a particularly spine-chilling demise.

"Anything on the other side of the island?" asks the husband.

That night, just before the big celebration is about to begin, Colonel Mike and Captain Billy show up at our door. Colonel Mike, a born opportunist, has heard about the makings of a free feast and wangled an invitation. "Really great of them, especially when they asked me to bring Captain Billy along," he enthuses. Both Linda and I are more than struck by the similarity between Captain Billy's flushed face and the evening's main course. The pair soon departs, eager to be first in line at the buffet.

They are wise to leave early. By the time we arrive, the smell of roast pork wafting along the shore has attracted a horde of revellers, and the food area is a mad scramble for plates and meat. "Everyone line up," hollers Mama Manu, who is wearing a floral print dress and a gardenia behind her right ear for the occasion. "There's enough for everyone."

Captain Billy has been partaking from a keg of free beer. "You heard the old sow," he shouts. "Line up, you lazy bastards."

Papa Manu, in the midst of slaking the baking pit with a pot of water, takes offence to the portly mariner's insult. "Hey, fatty," he challenges. "You want to eat supper, or you want to *be* supper?"

Captain Billy puffs out his large gut. "What you going to do about it?"

Papa Manu grins widely, in much the same manner his forebears no doubt greeted the first missionaries that ventured onto this beach. He turns and shouts something in Maori that bears a striking resemblance to "Come and get it!"

The result is dramatic. In addition to being a butcher, Papa Manu is also the captain of the local rugby team, and those few short words bring half a dozen stout lads running. The hapless sailor has only a few seconds to scream before his vocal cords are choked off by a pineapple and he is unceremoniously tossed into the pit. Fortunately for Captain Billy, Papa Manu has over-doused the pit, and he suffers little more than damage to his dignity. With the aid of Colonel Mike, he clambers out of the soggy pit and quickly scampers off, amid gales of laughter.

After dinner, plates and tables are cleared to make way for the band. A group of local musicians plays an impromptu set of reggae, as well as numerous island numbers featuring complex vocal harmonies and an electric ukulele. Regardless of the music, everyone favours the traditional island dance, which involves a lot of hip gyrations and arm movements. I heartily recommend avoiding doing "The Bump" with any woman weighing more than three hundred pounds.

By midnight, it seems that half the island is in attendance, and the joint is heaving. The adjacent main road is backed up for several hundred metres, as revellers abandon their cars and walk to the party. Empty bottles of Cooks Lager roll about underfoot, laid to rest where they have been consumed.

Sonny, the birthday boy, dances the night away with a pretty woman named Tiunu. Obviously very much infatuated with one another, they are just about to depart for some lip wrestling in the bushes when they are interrupted by the arrival of Sonny's fiancée. Sweet Susan, who shares the same dimensions as an upright piano, has arrived from the nearby island of Aitutaki as a birthday surprise. To say that Sonny is surprised is an understatement; horrified would be more accurate.

When Sweet Susan charges in his direction, I am impressed by his mobility in reverse gear. Unable to catch his rapidly retreating form, Sweet Susan instead turns her attention to Tiunu, grabbing a healthy fistful of her thick, raven black hair. To her credit, Tiunu gives as well as she gets. Although overmatched by a good fifty pounds, she is quick with her fists and the pair rolls energetically in the dirt, kicking and screaming, much to the delight of the mob. It is, in fact, the cheering that eventually attracts the attention of the police. Suspecting a cockfight, which has been declared illegal by Parliament, the cops arrive with motorcycle sirens wailing, igniting the crowd into another traditional Cook Island celebration, the Saturday night riot.

Linda and I decide it is time to retire to the Paradise Inn. We cut through the back of the Manus' yard, where we find Papa Manu, resting beside an empty barbecue pit, a quart of ale tucked tenderly in the crook of his arm.

"What did I tell you?" he muses, as we walk by. "Isn't it a bloody great party?" ▪

Chapter 2

Making a Racquet

Dawn on the Cook Islands is wondrous to behold. One moment, the night is all black, the silhouette of palms outlined by a million twinkling stars and the sweet, moist perfume of bougainvillea filling the air. The next, far to the east, the merest blush of deep violet graces the endless horizon and the breeze shifts from the mountainous cliffs to the sea, now carrying the sound of the distant surge pounding against the reef. A cock crows, and the blush of violet evaporates into a swiftly rising curtain of reddish orange that engulfs the sky as the new day bursts onto the world.

At least, that's what *usually* happens. The morning after Sonny's birthday party more accurately resembles *Dawn of the Dead*, with celebrants staggering like zombies down the road toward their homes. A cloud of smoke from the remnants of the scorched party tent drifts among the palm trees that dot Papa Manu's land, and the odour of urine-doused charcoal hangs in the air. The German couple, not even bothering to wait for a taxi, are dragging their hastily packed suitcases down the road as fast as they can.

As I decompress from the excitement of the night before, I sit down to learn about happenings elsewhere. The weekly *Cook Island News*, which is published every Friday in Avarua, features a wide assortment of thoroughly scandalous rumours and tasty recipes, with a few snippets of news thrown in to separate the ads. One of this week's nuggets describes how the minister for public morals has rather charitably allowed his mistress to inhabit a seaside home that is currently the property of the state. Another details the awarding of a rather generous rat-extermination contract to a local firm, whose primary qualification appears to be that the owner is the nephew of the minister of public safety. An account of the sea-cucumber infestation is accompanied by a curry recipe for same.

But all of this gripping news is secondary to the headline: the supply boat arrived yesterday! This may sound picayune, but the arrival of the supply boat is, without a doubt, the most anticipated event of the month for anyone who lives on an isolated island. During my visit last week to the main grocery store in Avarua, the aisles were empty of shoppers, and for good reason: all that was left on the shelves was row upon row of canned sardines in tomato sauce. Linda and I spent the last few days eating fish-bait pizza for dinner. But every four weeks or so, a tramp steamer from New Zealand pulls into port, bearing a wide variety of fresh and canned food, as well as shoe polish, toilet paper, and all the other niceties of civilization. I throw down the paper and immediately head for the door. As I walk into town, I pass the main harbour, where a squat, rusting ship rests beside the main dock. A pile of empty wooden pallets indicates that its contents have been disgorged and dispersed. I quicken my step; I want to get there before the best goodies are snatched up.

At the store, several dozen shoppers, all with big grins, are surging up and down the aisles, filling their carts with canned pumpkin, pink flip-flops, fresh cauliflower, and toothpicks. I merrily join in, purchasing a large quantity of pasta, a purple umbrella, two tins of boneless chicken, and, on impulse, an enormous turnip.

By the time I return to the Paradise Inn, most of Papa Manu's guests have departed and the smoke has dispersed. Violet, the hotel's maid, is busy sweeping away the leaves that have fallen from the bougainvillea and blown into the foyer. A native of the outlying island of Atiu, seventeen-year-old Violet possesses a sweet, shy disposition, so it is with some consternation that I notice a shiner over her left eye and her long, sad face. "Did you get into a fight last night?"

Violet instantly cheers up at the recollection. "I got into two!"

I nod in a fashion that I hope indicates this is indeed a reason for jollity. "So, if you got into *two* fights last night, why the long face?"

Violet's sad look returns, and she twists at a pink ribbon in her hair. "I don't have a boyfriend. I am worried I will be an old maid."

"Well, maybe if you didn't beat them up … ?" I offer.

"Oh, I never beat up boys! Just other girls."

I silently offer a blessing on behalf of the island's male population. "Well, if I run into any single boys, I'll let them know you're still available." This seems to help, as Violet thanks me and sets to sweeping with a new vigour.

I carry on to our room, with my purchases. Linda is quite pleased with the purple umbrella, as it will protect her from the heat of the day, but not with the turnip. "What are we supposed to do with the turnip?" she asks. "I hate turnip."

"Halloween is coming up. We could carve a Jack-o-lantern."

Linda rolls her eyes and tucks the turnip into the tiny fridge. "Maybe it will taste good with sardines."

After dropping off the groceries, my next task for the day is to register for the national squash championships, which I read about in the morning's newspaper. With all due modesty, I should note that I have been in demand as a squash team captain for many years (primarily because the responsibilities of the position include providing liquid refreshments after the match).

Karen says the island's one and only squash club is located west of Avarua, some ninety metres inland from the main road. I follow her directions exactly, but reach the end of the road without encountering anything remotely sporting. Fortunately, a young man leaning against his public-works shovel directs me back toward my destination. The club, which I had originally mistaken for a Second World War air-raid bunker, is a square, concrete building, decorated on the exterior by a riotous display of mould. Inside, the decor features several rickety wooden benches and a pop machine.

Even though it is a national championship, the girl behind the counter happily informs me that there are no limitations as to who can play; all are welcome. There are four categories in the competition, ranging from A to D. Since I have absolutely no idea of the level of competition, I decide to opt for the level starting my last name and choose C. The entrance fee is $9, which I pay with three $3 Cook Island coins. The girl gives me a receipt and tells me to return Saturday morning, a week from now.

As I am registering, someone addresses me from behind. "Up for a bit of a challenge, are you?" I turn, then look up—way up. My new acquaintance stands about six foot six and looks to be about 150 pounds. He is fair, with bright red hair, and speaks with a New Zealand accent. I don't have the slightest doubt he could stand mid-court and touch both side walls with his finger tips.

"I hope you're not in the competition," I say.

Des introduces himself and shakes my hand. "Don't worry about me. I just started playing a few months ago." He explains that he has lived here for the last few years, and he runs a construction company. "Where are you from?"

"Canada. We're here for a while. I thought I'd join up to meet some folks."

Des laughs. "Well, you came to the right spot. There're plenty of characters to meet here. What are you doing later this afternoon?" I admit that I don't have any plans. "Why don't you and your wife drop by my house for tea and meet my wife? She'd love to hear about Canada."

I readily agree, and after Des explains how to get to his home, I head back to let Linda know our plans. I find her standing in our room, dressed in a bikini, her head cocked to one side. "Shh," she says, as I enter. "Can you hear that?"

I glance carefully around. Our room is decorated in what I refer to as Raro chic. The walls are painted ivory and barnacled with woven baskets of indeterminate function. The floor is covered with sisal mats, and the couch and chair, which appear to have drifted in with the tide, are spruced up with a fabric that features a Polynesian geometric design. A circular, steel stairway leads up to the loft, where a low-hanging ceiling fan adds new meaning to the term "buzz cut." As far as I can tell, none of it is making a strange noise. "What am I supposed to be listening for?"

"There! Did you hear it?"

I did indeed. From somewhere in our room comes the tiny, mewling sound of a kitten. Since our arrival, a kitten with black face and white paws has adopted us, arriving promptly at breakfast and dinner. We have christened our little visitor "Trouble." I check under the couch and in the shower stall, but Trouble is nowhere to be found.

"What were you doing when you first heard her?" I ask.

Linda points to a bowl of chopped fruit on the kitchen table. "I just came in to get something to eat."

I glance at the tiny fridge that squats beside the kitchen sink. "Did you get it out of the fridge?"

Linda's eyes widen. She opens the door and Trouble nonchalantly steps out. She shudders once, then wanders out the door, wiping milk off her whiskers. Linda takes the nibbled container out and pours it down the drain. "I guess we'll need some more for tea, now," she moans, but she brightens up when I explain we've been invited to visit Des and his family. She changes into street clothes, and we're soon on our way.

Following Des's directions, we walk inland about half a kilometre. The streets of Avarua soon give way to farmland, which is divided into small plots. Many of them are covered with papaya and banana trees, and I can't help but notice that much of the fruit has fallen to the ground, where wandering piglets and chickens gorge upon the spoiled produce.

En route, we encounter Charlie, Karen's boyfriend. Charlie is a large, muscular man who carries himself gracefully, something common to Cook Islanders. He also exhibits a good wit and is a dab hand with a barbecue, a skill that I admire. When we spot him, he is standing, bare-chested, in the middle of a strip of wet, marshy ground, pounding a patch of low, wide-leaved plants with a long, wooden cudgel. We hail him and ask what he's doing. "Tending my taro patch," he explains.

I congratulate him on his industriousness and ask why nobody seems to be worrying about the fallen fruit.

"Oh, they planted those a few years ago, but there's no way to get them to market," Charlie says. "And who's going to spend money here on papaya when it's free for the asking?"

I mention that the rich, fertile soil might be put to better use growing market vegetables instead of having to wait for the monthly supply boat, but his face breaks out into a big, wide grin at the suggestion.

"All of the land here is owned communally, which means that nobody owns it. If I started a tomato patch, as soon as the crop was ready, everybody would come and help themselves because the land belongs to them just as much as me."

"Then how come you're growing a taro patch?"

"Cause it's bloody hard work to get it out of the ground." Charlie swings the heavy cudgel into the air and down into the wet ground, forcing a tuber to the surface. "They're too lazy to take it *all*!"

Des's home is on a rise, overlooking the fields. It is a simple house, with a low-pitched roof that extends out over a wide porch and large windows to let the cool onshore breeze pass through the interior. His wife, Tabita, greets us at the door. A native Cook Islander, she is slim, with dark hair, and possesses the same brilliant smile and happy nature as her compatriots. She is in her late twenties, a few years younger than Des, and wears a sleeveless cotton blouse, a colourful, patterned skirt, and a shell necklace. Her eyes sparkle with curiosity as she invites us in.

Des and Tabita's home is furnished with low couches and decorated with watercolours. Their one-year-old son, Roy, plays with a plastic toy shark on the wooden floor. Numerous tables are stacked with primary-school textbooks, reflecting Tabita's occupation as a teacher in the local school. She invites us to sit down, then disappears into the adjacent kitchen. She soon reappears with a tray of biscuits and tea, and joins Des and us in the living room. "Tell me about Canada," she asks.

"It's tough to even think about it when you live in paradise," I say. "You must love it here."

Des glances over at his wife. "Actually, we're thinking of moving to New Zealand."

"Why?" asks Linda.

Des picks up Roy and places him in his lap. "There simply isn't enough opportunity for the young. They grow up full of ambition, but only the lucky few can find jobs."

As we drink our tea, Tabita asks about our backgrounds. When I explain I am a geologist by training, she perks up. "You must come to my class and tell the children about the geology of Rarotonga."

I readily agree. If there is one thing I enjoy more than reading my own words, it's hearing my own voice. It is soon time for Roy's bath, and we make our farewells and head back to town, contemplating what to cook for dinner. I can only hope that Trouble hasn't eaten the turnip in the fridge.

Tabita's invitation piques my interest in learning more about the Cook Islands. The next day, I make a trip to the National Public Library, which is located about a half kilometre inland from the Paradise Inn on a quiet side road.

For a national library, the building is a rather modest, one-storey, cement affair of perhaps three hundred square metres. The interior sports a broad selection of mystery thrillers, crime dramas, and bodice rippers, but I also find a modest selection of reference books to peruse and settle in at a desk to learn more about my new home.

There are fifteen islands in the Cook Islands' group, a mix of coral atolls and extinct volcanoes scattered in a north-to-south arc, which runs fifteen hundred kilometres. It seems that the Cook Islands were settled sometime after AD 800 by adventurers from Tonga and Samoa. The Ara Metua, a highway paved in limestone blocks that once completely ringed Rarotonga, was built around AD 1100. The first European to visit the islands was Spanish navigator Alvaro de Mendaña de Neira, who spotted the northern island of Pukapuka in 1595. Although Captain James Cook arrived relatively late in the festivities, exploring many of the islands on his three voyages in 1773, 1774, and 1777, the entire group is named for him.

Captain Cook himself was a wonder. Born to a Yorkshire farming family in 1728, he ran away as a teenager and joined the merchant navy. He quickly rose through the ranks and, when the Seven Years War broke out between Britain and France, he joined the Royal Navy and participated in the siege of Québec, where his talent for surveying provided General Wolfe with the route to sneak up on the French forces and defeat them on the Plains of Abraham. After the war, Cook was commissioned by the Royal Society to map uncharted waters. Thanks to his endeavours, huge voids in the planet's geography were filled in, including New Zealand, Australia, and much of the west coast of Canada, before he was clubbed to death in the Hawaiian Islands in 1779 by cartography critics.

Speaking of hostile natives, the Cook Islanders hold the distinction of being the only Pacific inhabitants to ever eat a European woman. Ann Butchers (unfortunate name, that) was the girlfriend of the captain of the *Cumberland*, an Australian merchant boat that came to the islands looking for sandalwood. When the boat landed on the east coast of Rarotonga in 1814, a fight broke out between crew members and locals, which resulted in her death. Not wanting to waste a good meal, the Rarotongans baked her in a ground oven and served her up, no doubt, with a nice Merlot.

Cannibalism was eventually eliminated by John Williams, a

representative of the London Missionary Society, who arrived in 1821 and immediately set out to convert the natives from their seventy-one gods and twelve heavens to the more economical Trinity. By a cruel twist of fate (the sort, I must confess, that I thoroughly enjoy), some years later he became the main course for another group of gourmets in the New Hebrides.

The missionaries who replaced Williams ran the islands for the next sixty years, until the British established a protectorate in 1888. New Zealand then annexed the group in 1901. The Cook Islands gained independence in 1965, but relied heavily (and still do) upon help from its former masters. This aid, primarily in the form of annual funds, is a prime motivator for financial shenanigans, a skill at which Cook Islanders seem especially adept.

Reading about the Ara Metua inspires me to explore those parts of the ancient road that still exist beneath the current highway that circles the island. At more than thirty kilometres in length, it is a little too long to hike, and I don't trust the local scooter-rental agents any more than I'd trust a shark to trim my hair. I am still pondering the increasingly short list of transportation alternatives when I arrive back at the Paradise Inn. I spot a scooter parked behind the main office and, in a flash of inspiration, decide to see if Karen would lease me hers for a day.

I find her, dressed in a sarong, lying on a chaise lounge on the patio, smoking a cigarette and reading a paperback. "I don't mind lending it out, but you need to get a Raro licence first," she explains.

"Won't my Canadian driver's licence do?"

"Nope. It's the law."

I am about to ask why the mechanic near the Edgewater Resort rented me a scooter with no compunction, but I answer my own question: laws in Raro are interpreted by the Cook Islanders as general guidelines, not rules. It takes a good Canadian girl to stick to the straight and narrow. Following Karen's directions, I trudge into town to the main police station. The constable behind the desk confirms that I need to apply for a licence or face civil penalties of an unspecified, though very strict indeed, sort. I sigh and pay him three dollars for my test. He directs me out a side door.

The side yard in which I find myself is equipped with three bright-orange road cones, standing between two palm trees. Some folks get quite uptight about taking tests, but I've driven motorcycles all my adult life, so feel quite confident as the constable emerges, dressed in a reflective traffic vest and a pair of immense white-leather riding boots. He guides a scooter to one palm tree, parks it, and invites me to mount it. He then stands to one side, expectantly.

"What am I supposed to do now?" I ask.

"You must navigate the obstacle course." He takes a small clipboard and pen from his vest and waits with what I assume is a testing stance.

I am tempted to burst out laughing, but refrain. Obstacles, palm trees especially, are a bane to Cook Island drivers. In truth, collisions are the number two reason for palm tree destruction, just after monsoon winds. Just last weekend alone, according to the *Cook Island News*, five motorists struck palm trees, "all of them apparently sober." The drivers, that is, not the trees.

This is going to be a cakewalk. I kick-start the scooter, gun the throttle, and promptly fishtail the rear wheel and dump the bike. I grin sheepishly at the constable as he makes a note on his clipboard. I pick the bike up, dust myself off, and get back into the saddle. This time, I lay off the gas and pilot the scooter sedately through the sinuous track, careful to avoid a scrawny chicken pecking at the base of the second palm tree.

My miserable effort must have been sufficient. The constable dutifully checks off my results and escorts me back into the station, where he takes my picture and embosses it on an official driver's licence, before sealing the document in waterproof plastic. As I walk home, I stop to show it to several pedestrians, who compliment me on the exceptional likeness. I also pat several palm trees, reassuring them that they are safe until the next monsoon. At least, that is, from me.

By the time I return, Linda has packed a lunch and a beach towel for our journey along the historic Ara Metua. Karen rolls out her scooter and turns over the keys. "Be sure you're back before dark—there's no headlight," she advises. I wonder what else might be missing, like brakes, but I decide to hold my tongue. Linda ties her straw hat on with a bow, and off we set.

Much of the ancient Ara Metua is covered with asphalt, but patches of ancient limestone blocks occasionally poke through. The route wanders through luscious jungle, taro patches, banana plantations, and papaya orchards. The traffic consists mostly of dogs, naked children playing in mud puddles, and the occasional stray pig. There's nothing quite like the feeling of sailing along in the bright sun, the wind streaming through your hair, a glimpse of the ocean flashing between palm groves on one side and the impressive forest-clad cliffs on the other.

The ride puts me in a contemplative mood, and I begin to wonder about the origins of the road. Charlie mentioned that it was built by an ancient chief named Toi, but other than that, not much is known. Everyone agrees that the road is very useful for moving goods and people around the island, but could it also have had some clan significance, like the totemic statues of Easter Island? Or perhaps it was built for defensive purposes, to move warriors quickly around the island to repel seaborne invaders. I guess I'm used to the Trans-Canada Highway, with its periodic signposts pointing out The Big Nickel or Skunk Cabbage Hollow, but I'm still somewhat surprised there are no plaques detailing the history of the Ara Metua along our way.

A half-dozen birds dart across the road, and I refocus my attention on the traffic. We motor along for several more kilometres until we come to Muri Beach, a largely deserted expanse of white sand that stretches more than a kilometre along the east end of the island. The barrier reef touches land on the north side of the beach, then extends in a wide arc, enclosing a shallow, brackish lake, about a half-kilometre wide at its greatest extent. We are alone, except for a fisherman who poles a flat-bottomed canoe across the lake, stopping occasionally to impale a fish.

We park the scooter and set up camp beneath the shade of a palm tree. I strip down to my swimming trunks and don a snorkel, mask, and pair of flippers that Karen has lent me. I ease into the warm waters and focus on the panorama below. My first discovery is an abundance of sea cucumbers, which I initially mistake for used condoms. Spiky black anemones, clinging to chunks of coral, also abound, as do tiny fish of a brilliant blue hue. I am bobbing gently in the swell, intently eyeing a form of coral called Spanish Dancer, a red-speckled blanket that undulates in the gentle pull of the tide, when I get the uncomfortable feeling that I am being watched. Turning abruptly, I find about three hundred brilliant-yellow parrot fish have quietly crept up behind me to see what I'm staring at. They immediately turn as one and face off in a different direction. I turn around and paddle a short distance, and they eagerly follow me like puppies waiting for a milk bone. It would be charming if it weren't so, well, weird, and I flipper back to shore.

I arrive just as the fisherman approaches. He is carrying his spear in one hand and a very large, very ugly fish in the other. Temu introduces himself and asks where we are from.

"We're from Canada," replies Linda.

"Canada! How old are you?" We are treated to a barrage of questions from Temu, including where are we staying, how long have we been in the Cooks, and where we are going afterward, until I finally cut in. I could have asked him about his family, or his clan, or maybe even his favourite holiday, but I am transfixed by the impressive hideousness of his catch. "Are you going to cook that for supper?"

"Oh, no! I'm going to sell it to the Flame Tree Restaurant." Temu rubs his tummy. "They cook delicious food. You must try it."

We agree, and, after helping him load his canoe onto a rickety pickup truck, follow him north along the coast for some ten kilometres. He slows and turns into a parking lot adjacent to the Flame Tree Restaurant, and we follow him in and park the scooter near the entrance. The Flame Tree is in a shady glade adjacent to the beach, a low building of traditional wooden planks and thatched roof, raised about two metres off the sandy ground by pilings.

While Temu heads out back to the kitchen, we follow a boardwalk from the parking lot to the front door. Inside, we are greeted by the hostess, Doris, who escorts us to a table. We tell her about Temu and his fish, and she laughs. "When you're on an island, you never know what the special of the day is until it arrives."

"What do you recommend tonight?" I ask.

"Try the *eke* for a starter. It's octopus cooked in tomato and coriander sauce and served on rice. We also have some fresh lamb just flown in from New Zealand."

We go with her suggestions. The octopus is a little chewy, but the rack of lamb, baked in a herb crust and served with roast potatoes and honey mint sauce, is superb. We wash it down with a Merlot from the Marlborough region in New Zealand. As we are finishing our meal, Doris rejoins us. "How do you like Raro?" she asks.

"The people here are very friendly and curious. Temu asked us a thousand questions."

Doris laughs. "Actually, it's more boredom than anything else. Living on an island makes you nosy about newcomers."

We thank Doris and head out to the parking lot. Night has fallen and the sky is overcast, and I am surprised by the darkness. I suddenly recall Karen's warning about the scooter's headlamp. I go back in and explain my problem to Doris, who, fortunately, has a flashlight I can borrow.

"I'll bring it back tomorrow," I promise.

"There's no rush. Just leave it with Karen and I'll pick it up in a few days. Just have a safe trip back." That's something I love about Raro, the way that everyone automatically trusts another person, even a total stranger.

We set out, Linda shining the flashlight over my shoulder while I drive, manoeuvring back and forth between the palm trees that line the road. I am about to silently congratulate myself on my ingenuity when it begins to rain. A curtain of water comes rushing up the road and soaks us to the skin in seconds. The scooter begins to cough, and we sputter along, the flashlight flickering on and off, until we finally spot the porch light of the Paradise Inn. We pull in and park the scooter, then head for our room, shivering.

Trouble is waiting at the front door for her dinner. She takes one look at us and sniffs, no doubt ashamed to be associated with people too simple-minded to come in out of the rain.

The National Squash Tournament is held the next day, Saturday. That morning, as I take my coffee out to the Paradise Inn's patio overlooking the ocean, the concrete is still wet from the previous night's rainstorm. The clouds have drifted off and the skies are clear, however, and I mention to Karen that it looks like it's going to be a pleasant day.

"Just wait until the sun starts to beat down on the club," she retorts. "It's going to be a sauna in there."

By mid-afternoon, when I arrive for my first match, the indoor court is not only sweltering, but has also taken on a delicate aroma that consists of equal parts gym sock and jockstrap. My first opponent, a young man whose immense size promises great potential on the rugby field, succumbs to my limited skills in three quick games. My second opponent is Doris from the Flame Tree Restaurant, who shows some skill but is more interested in maintaining her coiffure than going for the jugular. She, too, quickly passes to the consolation round.

By this time, I have worked up a tremendous thirst, to the point I am seriously contemplating taking a sip from a ratty, rusty tap jutting from a coarse cement wall. A young man named Chops rescues me from certain dysentery, however.

"Here, let me get you something," he offers. My new friend, who is about five feet tall and two hundred pounds, fetches a plastic bottle of frozen water from the club fridge. "Don't drink it all at once or you'll get a tremendous headache," he cautions. I gratefully massage my forehead with the icy beverage, until it melts enough to begin sipping.

"You have an interesting name," I venture. "Is it a traditional island handle?"

"No, it's short for my nickname, Porkchop. I'm a chef." Porkchop is obviously proud of his profession. "I invented a new dish, pork and pineapple tortillas."

The club clerk, without looking up from her movie-star magazine, speaks up. "He's a cook at the airport."

Chops ignores her, striking a pose as though he is about to leap into the air. "I'm also a champion island dancer."

"You eat his food and you'll be a champion island dancer too— at the trots."

Chops bursts into laughter. "Don't listen to her. Come on, you can watch me thrash my opponent."

"Who are you playing?"

Chops taps me on the chest. "You."

For the next forty minutes, Chops chases me around the court. He has the edge in youth and stamina, but I hold the balance in cunning and guile. We play all five games, and I finally win, three games to two in overtime, becoming a national champion in my class for the first (and only) time. There is no trophy, only bragging rights, but I feel like a million bucks.

Chops is gracious about his loss, fetching me another frozen water before we step around to the men's locker room for a quick, refreshing shower. I ask a bit about his upbringing. He tells me he was born and raised in Raro, and after graduating from high school, went to live with relatives in New Zealand. He returned when his father arranged a job for him in Avarua.

"Would you have preferred to stay in New Zealand?" I ask.

"Oh, no! I missed my family and friends—I got homesick."

By the time we return from showering, the main court has been wiped down and a long table is set up in the large room. "What's this for?" I ask.

"We always have a victory banquet afterward," explains Chops. Doris and several other women arrive, carrying platters from which tempting aromas emanate. A truck pulls up sporting a keg of beer on the flatbed, its aluminum skin shiny with condensation. A lad quickly installs a tap and begins pouring pitchers of the cold nectar, handing out plastic pint glasses to all and sundry.

I spot Des and go over to congratulate him on his win in the A division. Linda, Tabita, and Roy join us, and we proceed to the buffet together. As we walk along the table, Linda and I recognize dishes of pork cooked in coconut cream, grilled *mai-mai* or dolphin fish, and mashed taro, but several others elude us. Linda points to a creamy concoction that vaguely resembles custard. "What's that?"

"That's *poke*," explains Tabita. "It's baked banana in coconut cream. It's very sweet, and you can eat it as dessert."

Beside it stands a serving dish filled with bundled leaves. "And that?" asks Linda.

"That's *rakau*." Tabita takes a bundle and unties the string on top. "You bake a mixture of onions, meat, and coconut cream in the *rakau* leaf. It's lovely."

We load up our plates and it is all quite delicious, especially when washed down with cold lager. I am contemplating seconds, when the dishes and long table are quickly cleared away and replaced by a ring of chairs. The first young man whom I had handily beaten enters, carrying a ukulele, and takes a seat, along with three teenage girls. They smile to everyone and, without further ado, break into song.

I have never heard anything like a Cook Island ballad, and it takes my breath away. They sing, he alto and the girls soprano, in their native dialect, with only the ukulele to accompany them. Their sweet, angelic harmonies soar around the bare, concrete room like aural doves. I have no idea if they are love songs or tales of ancient deeds of derring-do, and, indeed, am so enraptured I have no idea how long they sing, only returning to Earth when they finish and take a bow to thunderous applause.

Des and Tabita soon depart to take Roy home. I exit the court and pull deeply on the night air. I am distracted by a hiccup and turn to see Chops sitting in the dirt, his back pressed against the wall of the club. He is clutching a pitcher of beer and has a decidedly hangdog look about him. "What's wrong, not enjoying the party?" I ask.

"No."

"Why not?"

"I'm sad."

"Sad?" I stare up at a million twinkling stars, as a warm breeze blows in from the shore and his pals whoop it up nearby. "What's there to be sad about? You've got a good job and you live in paradise."

Chops sniffs. "I don't have a girlfriend." He points off in the vague direction of some bushes, from which come giggles and laughter. "All my pals have girlfriends."

"Don't worry, you'll find a girlfriend soon, too."

He waves his hand, slopping some of the lager from the pitcher. "Are *you* going to find me one?"

A light bulb goes on in my head. "As a matter of fact, yes."

"Who?"

"Her name is Violet."

Chops brightens immediately. "You mean Violet from the Paradise Inn?"

"The same."

Chops slumps down again. "She must have a dozen boyfriends."

"I know for a fact she doesn't. She was asking me just the other day if I might introduce her to a nice single boy. You can do until I find one."

Now, before you accuse me of altruism, I should point out that I am not inspired by Cupid but rather by the immense potential for social mishap. I recalled my dating days when raging hormones would inspire me to go to desperate lengths, like the time I decided that taking a young lady named Chrissy on a romantic picnic in an isolated spot would be the ideal seduction scenario. I packed a bottle of Mateus rosé and a picnic blanket and drove her, via motorcycle, to a glade in the Rural Conservation Area outside Hamilton, Ontario. The glade was usually deserted because it could only be reached by foot; a bar placed across the lane kept cars from advancing any farther. Without thinking, I drove up to the barrier and ducked— Chrissy didn't. Fortunately, she wasn't hurt when she was knocked off the bike, but I was mortified. I figured if I could suffer such cringe-making faux pas, why shouldn't Porkchop?

At any rate, he takes the bait, rising from the dirt and shaking my hand. "Thank you, that's great!"

"No problem. I'll let her know you're going to call and invite her out."

Suddenly, his cheer disappears. "I couldn't do that! Not all alone!"

"Why not?"

"I'm too shy with girls. Would you and Linda come along? Please, please!"

How can I refuse a front-row seat to the festivities? I reluctantly promise that Linda and I will accompany him and Violet on their first date. Chops is so happy that he jumps behind the wheel of the flatbed truck and races off into the night. A posse of his friends immediately erupts from the bush, waving and shouting encouragement as the truck's tail lights disappear down the lane. Or maybe they were just mad because he took off with the beer keg. They're an excitable lot that way. ■

CHAPTER 3

A Date with Porkchop

The first day of October is, to put it precisely, gorgeous. The temperature sits somewhere around twenty-eight degrees Celsius, the sky is a brilliant sapphire blue, and the breeze wafting between the swaying palms carries the aroma of jasmine. It's a perfect day, in other words, to sit all day in the library.

It's my own fault, really. My talk to Tabita's class on the geology of Raro looms. Normally, I might just dash something off the top of my head—pull it out of nothing, as it were—but I'll be speaking in a school founded by missionaries and I'd feel a little shameful making it up completely. As it is, the library is somewhat bereft of geological texts, but I find an *Encyclopedia Britannica* that looks like it came over in Captain Cook's bilge hold and manage to flesh out enough details to hopefully bamboozle an eight year old.

Taking a break from my cramming, I find the library is hosting a presentation ceremony for the local spelling-bee champion. The girl, aged thirteen or so, stands shyly in her Sunday best, holding a ribbon. A tall, balding man with a very red complexion is taking her picture. After they are done, I approach and introduce myself to what I presume is the local news photographer. Mark is not only the shutterbug, but also the reporter, editor, and janitor of the *Cook Island News*, the authoritative journal of all things Raro and beyond. I compliment him on his comprehensive coverage of a nation spread over an area the size of India, although somewhat less populated, with, at most, eighteen thousand people.

"I have a lot of volunteer correspondents," he replies. "That's a nice way of saying everyone loves to gossip."

I join Mark as he walks back into town, and we stop at that universal gathering place for journalists, the local watering hole.

"If there's one thing that Cook Islanders love more than gossip, it's a scandal," he explains, as he sips his cold lager. Although, like everywhere else, the Cooks have had their share of shady Internet companies offering pornographic gambling and other such delights, their most famous scandal involves the development of the Sheraton Hotel. The two-hundred-unit mega resort was scheduled to open several years ago, but the partially finished project still huddles like the bones of a beached cement whale on the west coast of the island, about ten kilometres from the Paradise Inn.

It seems that the Italian developer contracted to build the thirty-million-dollar hotel went bankrupt, taking with him about twenty million dollars worth of luxury hotel materials to whereabouts unknown. The Cook Islands' government, which put up about one third of its annual budget to get the project off the ground, had to scramble to cover their collective butts. Intervening years of cyclone disasters, economic meltdowns, and generally short memories have left the project languishing in limbo, except for one week every year when Mark splashes a picture of the moss-covered remnants across the front page of the *Cook Island News*, accompanied by an editorial that dredges up the embarrassing facts in excruciating detail.

"They must love you around here," I say.

"The prime minister has a joke he loves to tell," Mark says. "What's the difference between a dead dog on the road and a dead reporter?"

"I don't know."

"There are skid marks in front of the dog."

At this point, you may be wondering why a person with an education in geology, like me, would abandon such a lucrative career to become something even politicians look down their noses at. Curiously, it was neither venality nor gross incompetence. Actually, I quite like the earth sciences, and while I did not excel in an academic sense, I had a firm grasp of the two fundamentals necessary to succeed in the profession: the ability to grow a beard and to drink alcohol to excess. Over the course of five years at the University of Waterloo, in Ontario, I learned enough about geology to land a job that involved indoor work and no heavy lifting. And I might have stayed there forever had I not sold a travel story about Macau to a newspaper and realized that people would actually pay me for something I *loved* to do.

A few days later, on Saturday night, Porkchop shows up at our room at the Paradise Inn. He is wearing his best Sunday clothes: an All Blacks rugby shirt, neon green surfing shorts, and flip-flops. He hands Linda a bouquet of lilies that he has plucked from a ditch on the way over and glances around our room. "Is Violet here yet?"

Linda places the lilies into a vase of water. "No, she's just finishing up. She said she'd be along in a few minutes."

Porkchop sits on the edge of the couch, but almost immediately bounces upright when a guest in an adjacent room passes our door. "You all right?" I ask.

"Sure." Porkchop flashes an unsure grin. "Just a little nervous, that's all."

I pat him on the back. "Don't worry, everything will be fine."

Actually, I'm beginning to worry a bit, myself. Ever since I approached Violet a few days ago and mentioned, as casually as possible, that Linda and I would like to ask her out along with my friend Porkchop, she has been equally on edge, alternating between delirious joy and unequivocal dread. "What if I say something wrong? What if he doesn't like me?" My enthusiasm for initiating Porkchop's social meltdown has waned, and the thought of being in the same room as the two of them for the whole evening sounds as inviting as riding in the back end of a cement truck.

Before I can incite Porkchop into fleeing, however, Violet arrives. Her hair, glistening with pomade, is perfectly coiffed, and her purple skirt and white T-shirt, with "Jeep" emblazoned across the chest, are stunningly complemented by a bright orange-silk shawl, draped over her shoulders. Porkchop instantly stops fidgeting and, taking the lilies out of the vase, rushes over to present them to her. Violet accepts his dripping gift and thanks him. Porkchop breaks into a big grin. "Well, what are we waiting for, let's get going!"

As we saunter into town, I take Porkchop by the elbow and walk ahead, out of earshot. "Have you thought about what we should do this evening?"

"You bet. My cousin April is in charge of the Playhouse ticket booth tonight. She said she'd let us in free to tonight's show."

The Playhouse in Avarua is the largest cinema in the Cook Islands. It is also the only one. Housed in a large, rusty Quonset hut, it features a screen stitched together from a half-dozen bedsheets, several hundred seats rescued from various ship sinkings and plane crashes, and some of the best popcorn to be found in the South Pacific.

The marquee announces that tonight's show is a Richard Gere movie. He is, without a doubt, my favourite star in the whole world—not for his acting skills, of course, but for his ability to preserve my sanity. You see, I suffer from suspension of disbelief on a world-class scale, which in itself is no bad thing, especially when I'm watching a film written by talented screenwriters, helmed by distinguished directors, and portrayed by serious actors. If, however, I happen to fall prey to some turgid turkey and find myself in danger of wanting to rescue a high-class prostitute and teach her to act like a proper lady, I can always count on Richard, the leading man, to come along and rescue me. With a pearly smirk and a cheery wink, he immediately de-suspends my disbelief, and I realize that he really isn't some businessman trying to save a hooker—it's all fake! I can't think how many times he has saved me thus, other than in every film I've ever seen him in. Thank you, Richard.

Cousin April is manning the booth, along with her dog, Sharky, a scruffy looking mutt of indeterminate lineage, and she waves us through. Although it is hot and muggy outside, large ceiling fans manage to stir up sufficient breeze to make the interior comfortably cool. Already, about five or six dozen people are scattered about the room, sitting and chatting with friends in advance of the film. While Linda and Violet pick out our seats, Porkchop and I make our way to the concession counter.

Unfortunately, it has been several weeks since the last supply ship docked and the Playhouse is out of popcorn. Instead, Porkchop buys four chocolate-dipped ice cream cones, and we make our way back to the seats. He squeezes into the centre of the row with Violet, while Linda and I take the aisle seats. I pick some dried kelp off the armrest of my chair and settle in. The lights dim and, after several slide commercials for local restaurants and the Banana Bar, the main program begins.

Tonight, Richard plays a rebel soldier who comes home from prison after the Civil War. His wife (played by Jodie Foster) isn't sure if it's him or not, but since he seems to know a lot about how to pucker up and kiss, and he's such a hunk, she figures, what the hell, might as well take him for a spin.

Obviously, Jodie doesn't get the pearly-smirk-and-wink business, but I do, so I am cheerily ignoring the movie and watching everyone else, when something plants a cold, wet nose on the back of my bare leg. I let out a shriek and throw my ice cream into the air. It lands with a wet splat in the aisle, which, apparently, is what Sharky intended in the first place, as he immediately lunges upon his prey, devouring it in a single gulp before it has any chance of escape. Licking his chops, he glides off beneath the seats in search of his next victim.

My shriek, though blood-curdling, has failed to attract the attention of the projectionist, who has obviously left the building. About forty-five minutes into the movie, the reel ends with a *gwark* from Richard, and he and Jodie are replaced with a blinding white screen. April is sent off to look for the projectionist, who is finally located smooching with his gal out back. He eventually returns and loads the next reel into the projector, and the movie resumes.

It seems that Porkchop has been waiting for this moment to make his move. Doing an elaborate stretch, he casually places one arm over Violet's shoulder. Violet, her eyes on the screen, feigns not to notice, but I can see her lips curl up in the tiniest smile. Porkchop, grinning widely, leans back and winks at me across the back of the seats.

I return my attention to the movie but, a few moments later, I am distracted by a vague movement out of the corner of my eye. I glance over toward Porkchop, who is silently waving his free arm in the air to attract my attention. I give him a silent *What?* and he points in the vague direction of his left arm, draped over Violet's shoulder.

I instantly spot the reason for his concern. The tassel edging of Violet's shawl is caught in the expandable strap of Porkchop's wrist-watch, and he cannot move for fear of ripping the material.

Porkchop, by now, is in a panic: *What should I do?* I make a vague motion to suggest he embrace her, and perhaps then he can reach over and free himself. His eyes widen and he shakes his head: *No.* I shrug in Gallic fashion: *What else can you do?* Porkchop rolls his eyes in resignation and reaches over.

In order to appreciate what happens next, you have to understand that Violet is very large in the chest area and Porkchop's arms are woefully short for the task of bridging it. Violet, concentrating on Richard's semi-exposed butt bouncing around in Jodie's bed, has been completely oblivious to all the goings-on until she suddenly discovers Porkchop taking what appears to be liberties with her bust. She leans back and cracks him soundly with a left hook, then stands and flees the theatre. As soon as his vision has cleared, Porkchop jumps up and rushes after her, the silk scarf trailing from his wrist like a distress signal.

Linda and I belatedly follow them out into the street, but they have disappeared into the darkness. Since we have no idea where they've gone, and Richard's misadventures have lost their appeal at the moment, we decide, upon consideration, that the best plan is to go to the Banana Bar.

By this time, the Banana Bar is in full Saturday-night mode.

The low building is packed to the rafters, and people are spilling out through the windows. Although a line of people is waiting at the front door, Charlie, a man of many talents, is working as bouncer for the evening and he lets us in.

We squeeze into a booth with Karen, who is sitting with one of the other guests from the Paradise Inn: Sven, a Swedish biker, with Harley tattoos all over his arms. It's noisy in the bar and his accent is a bit thick, but from what I can understand, he is part of a crew sailing a private yacht from New Zealand to San Diego. We are interrupted by the arrival of several pitchers of the house specialty, banana daiquiris, which turn out to be very refreshing in the sweltering heat.

We have hardly had a chance to consume more than two or three pitchers when Tiny Sparrow, the guest performer for the evening, takes to the stage. He is a slightly built man, almost wiry, who sports a knit Rasta cap, dark shades, and a sleeveless leather vest and whose beautiful singing voice would do any Islander proud. After a few traditional chorales, he and his band break down into a funky reggae beat that soon has the floor full of dancers.

Now, generally, I am too retiring and shy to get up on the dance floor, but the banana daiquiris seem to have an invigorating effect, and when Sven urges me to demonstrate some indigenous Canadian dances, I decide to show the crowd a few moves that once won me honourable mention at a chiropractors' convention. I give them the Rocky Mountain Rumba and the Saskatoon Shuffle, and soon, everyone who isn't overcome with laughter gets into the act, adding their own flourishes to the festivities. Tiny Sparrow improvises a reggae rap on the spot, and the bar sends over another round of pitchers on the house. The joint is soon so packed that we can't even move, which is just as well, as I am thoroughly beyond even attempting to dance. I vaguely recall practising my pearly wink on Linda, before she hauls me out through a window, the only available egress, and carries me home.

There is no sign of either Violet or Porkchop for the next several days. I spend the time lying in the sun and gradually drying out before the day of my guest lecture at Tabita's school arrives. At the appointed hour, I don my finest Hawaiian shirt and dress shorts, tuck my notes under my arm, and head out along the main road.

We have been staying at the Paradise for slightly over a month, and I now know quite a few people in the neighbourhood. As I lope along at Raro speed, my sandals making a happy *flap-flap* noise against the hot asphalt, I wave to Mama Ti as she lays out a display of papaya in front of her grocery store. Some lads from the squash tournament shout "Hullo," as they roar past in the back of a pickup truck. Two women smile as I pass and begin to do a ludicrous jig that seems strangely familiar. It is good to be alive.

The school is located a few blocks inland from the main road. It is a series of low huts situated at one end of an immense playing field, which is surrounded by a wire-mesh fence that keeps goats from eating the rugby turf. I enter the main building and ask the school secretary for the whereabouts of Tabita's class, and she directs me to the end of the hallway.

The classroom is large and airy; windows almost completely cover one wall. A covered walkway outside shelters the room from the day's heat, and only a cool breeze penetrates the shady interior. The front wall supports a large chalkboard, and maps of the Cook Islands and the world hang on the other walls, along with paper cutouts of palm trees, mangoes, and sharks.

The pupils, perhaps thirty of them, all dressed in white shirts and dark shorts, shout out a greeting in unison when Tabita introduces me. She explains that I'm from Canada, and I will be lecturing on the geology of the Cook Islands. They take out notebooks and wait, pencils clutched in hand, attentive.

The age of the class ranges somewhere from twelve to fourteen years, so I decide to keep the technical explanation to a minimum. I draw a rough sketch of a cross-section of the earth on the chalkboard to explain the inner workings of the planet.

In order to understand the geological history of these islands, I tell the kids, you need to go back to the very beginning of this planet.

As best as scientists can reckon, blobs of solar dust coalesced to form Earth a little over 4.5 billion years ago. Shortly after its birth, the first continents emerged from the very young oceans. Today, although some ancient snippets of those continents still exist, virtually all the ocean bottom is much, much younger, in the order of 200 million years, at most.

This vast difference in ages is due to plate tectonics. For countless eons, the continents and ocean bottom have been sliding around on an inner layer of molten rock due to the emergence of magma along great ridges that bisect the oceans. This new rock expands the skin of the earth by a few centimetres a year—that's what pushed the continents of Africa and South America apart. But since the earth's surface is limited in size, an equal amount of real estate has to be consumed somewhere else. A lot of this happens in the Pacific Ocean, around what is known as the Ring of Fire. This volcano- and earthquake-prone line, which runs roughly around the rim of the Pacific, is where oceanic rock plunges beneath the continents in subduction zones and gets re-melted. Movement along the Ring of Fire is very slow, but inexorable, and millions of years from now, California will be pushed north until Disneyland sits adjacent to Alaska. I know Mickey will be pleased.

So what does all this have to do with the Cook Islands? Although no mid-ocean ridges lurk in their vicinity, a very ancient "hotspot" exists nearby. A hotspot is an area in the earth's inner molten layer that persists for long periods of time, warming the ocean crust above it to the point where it melts and forms a volcano that, like a giant pimple, breaks to the surface. Since the ocean plate is moving, however, the volcano eventually becomes extinct and is replaced by a new eruption. This process creates a string of volcanic islands that act as signposts for the plate's movements. The process can be seen in action in the Hawaiian Island chain, where the oldest, dormant volcanoes form islands to the northwest, and the youngest, active volcanoes form islands to the southeast.

For whatever reason, the hotspot beneath the Cooks is no longer producing volcanoes. The volcanic basalt of the older islands to the north and west, such as Manihiki and Suwarrow, has long since been eroded to below sea level, and all that can be seen are the coral reefs that have grown apace with the submerging volcanoes to create low, limestone islands.

The basaltic backbone of Raro still sticks above water, however, creating the sawtoothed ridge that runs down the centre of the island. The island's maximum elevation is 652 metres above sea level, but the island itself rises nearly 4,000 metres from the sea bottom, as high as the tallest peaks in North America. Millions of years from now, Raro will join the rest of its cousins as a low atoll, the waves of the Pacific lapping over the school.

Tabita's students listen silently and politely, until I am done. "Does anyone have any questions?"

A girl with pink ribbons in her hair sticks up her hand. "Is it true it gets so cold in Canada your bare skin sticks to metal?"

I am at first surprised by the question because it has nothing to do with the lesson, but I recall Tabita mentioning how insatiably curious the children are about the outside world.

"Yes, it's true." I tell them the story about when I was five and an older boy, Donny, made me put my tongue on the metal swing behind our elementary school at recess. "It got stuck and I couldn't get free. When the bell rang, Donny started laughing and ran back in and left me there all alone."

"What happened?" asks the girl with pink ribbons.

"The principal finally came looking for me. When he saw I was stuck, he went back to his office and got out a bottle of Scotch and poured it on my tongue and that loosened it up."

I speak of tobogganing, making snow angels, and digging out snow forts, wearing the woolen mittens and hat my grandmother knit, then coming home, soaking and cold, and my mother making me hot chocolate with marshmallows in it. The mechanics of plate tectonics are forgotten. When I mention sighting polar bears in the backyard, however, Tabita decides that the kids have heard enough lectures for one day. She hauls out some stiff, white cardboard and a box of scissors, and we spend the next hour cutting snowmen and decorating the walls. I must say, they look very nice among the sharks, and I compliment everyone on my wonderful visit before taking my leave.

It's a glorious thing, educating the young.

When they say that all good things must come to an end, apparently, they are specifically referring to indolence. It is almost 6:00 PM, and Linda and I are sitting on the patio of the Paradise Inn, watching the sun dip into the Pacific Ocean. We are sipping cocktails made from Charlie's *mangai* brew, something he whips up in a still behind his taro patch. According to Charlie, it is nothing more than fermented pineapple and orange juice, but he has a glint in his eye when he hands us the glasses, and I wonder if he's spiced it up with windscreen fluid or Aqua Velva.

I take a sip—it's not bad for moonshine—then turn my attention to a minor detail of paperwork, namely, our thirty-day visas expired a week ago. It seems that, what with the endlessly beautiful days and languid nights, we lost track of such things. Being slightly anal, I am a tad worried we might be hauled away by the visa patrol and tossed into the brig, or whatever they call it hereabouts. "Do you think I should go to the airport and try to renew them?" I ask.

Linda takes a sip of her drink. "No, I think it's time to move on."

I scratch my head, perplexed. The weather is ideal, the beaches immaculate, and we've met nice friends and had a fun time. "I must be missing something here. We're sitting on a tropical island with absolutely nothing to do except laze around all day and you want to leave?"

"I'm tired of lying around. I want something to *do*."

"Like, what?"

"Like theatre and shows and all the things that a big city has to offer. I want more *action*."

I have to admit, we've seen most of the attractions that the island offers, and I could swear I've read almost every book in the library. And, as fun as it was talking to the school kids, I didn't see it as a long-term occupation. With a start, I realize that, as beautiful as the surroundings are, Linda is right—we both need something more. "I never thought I'd be unhappy in paradise."

Karen appears on the patio with her cup of coffee and settles in beside us on a lounge chair. "You've got island fever."

"What?"

"It's like cabin fever, only you get it being stuck out here in the middle of nowhere." She waves a hand in the general direction of the Pacific, which stretches to the horizon in all directions. "You reach the point where you think you're going crazy."

"How do you cope with it?" I ask.

Karen tips her cup. "A big shot of Kahlua helps, but there's only one cure."

"What's that?"

"Get your ass to Sydney."

Linda nods. "I'll call the travel agent tomorrow."

Our plane leaves for Sydney, Australia, the following Sunday. In honour of our departure, Karen decides to hold a going-away party the night before. "No riot, just a few friends," she promises, and we are greatly relieved. Our departure plans consist of packing two small, carry-on bags, tidying up our room, and emptying the fridge. Trouble is more than happy to drink the remaining milk.

At the appointed hour, Des and Tabita arrive with Roy in tow, the latter happy to chase after the cat while the adults visit. Tabita has brought a gift, a string of shells. She places the necklace around Linda's neck and kisses her on the cheek. "It is an old tradition, giving it to friends. Once you have it, you always come back."

We go to the patio, where Charlie has fired up the grill and is busy seasoning a large plate of steaks. After a month of pork, fish, and chicken, my mouth begins to water at the sight. "Those look great," I say.

Charlie beams. "They're fresh today."

"Did the supply boat come in early?"

"No, it's Mama Manea's milk cow. It got hit by the bus." He pokes one of the steaks. "Nice and tender, eh?"

We eat the steaks with mashed taro and boiled greens from Charlie's plot, washing it all down with a glass of wine. After dinner, Karen brings out a pineapple cake she baked just for the occasion, complete with a stylized Canadian flag, done in maraschino cherries, and a sparkler.

By this time, Violet has forgiven me for setting her up with Porkchop and shows up with several girlfriends and a case of beer tucked under her arm. We play the Raro version of *Trivial Pursuit*, in which participants must down a shot glass of Charlie's homebrew after each incorrect answer. Sven, the Swedish biker, is soon so drunk that he starts to sing Scandinavian ballads, or moose calls—it's difficult to tell which. He eventually picks up Trouble and wanders off for a nap beneath the fuchsia.

Several other friends drop in to say goodbye, but as the evening wears on, I am concerned that Porkchop has failed to put in an appearance. I'd at least like the chance to tease him a bit. I take Karen aside. "Is he still mad at me for trying to set him up on a date with Violet?"

"No, I just think he had to work tonight."

"That's a shame. I was hoping to say goodbye to him."

Karen holds up a four-litre bladder of wine. "Well, at least we can toast his absence."

Charlie chimes in. "I want to toast Fred."

"Who's that?" I ask.

"He's the rooster that *cock-a-doodle-doos* next door every morning at four."

I raise my glass. "What do you want to say?"

"I don't want to *say* anything." Charlie points to the grill. "I just want to toast the damn thing."

Violet and her friends sing a few ballads of ancient heroes and dangerous voyages, which makes me very sad and thirsty. Slowly at first, then somewhat faster, the wine bladder collapses. I vaguely recall pledges of eternal friendship and inviting everyone, including Fred, to come and visit us someday in Calgary, before Linda drags me off to bed.

The next thing I know, the alarm is clattering, my head is aching, and my mouth feels as though it has played host to a weasel convention. I reach over and slap the alarm clock off the night table, and it comes to rest somewhere on the floor, still ringing. I clamber out and finally locate it under the bed—it's 3:00 AM, time to leave for the airport. We splash water on our faces, get dressed, and then go out to the front desk, where our taxi awaits.

"Hey, how are you my friend?" asks Pawpaw, a big grin on his face.

"I thought Tony drove the taxi at night."

"Oh no, he drives it in the day now."

"What happened to his ambulance job?"

Pawpaw smacks his hands together. "Boom! Hit a palm tree. Now we got no more ambulance."

We head out. The only thing moving in downtown Avarua is a scrawny chicken, but the airport is a hive of activity. Cabs and buses from all over the island are arriving, bringing in ongoing travellers and awaiting the new influx.

We check in at the airline counter and make our way toward the departure gate. The customs agent, a woman of about twenty-five, has, without a doubt, the most humourless expression I have seen in my entire stay on the island. She glances at our passports. "Do you realize that your visas expired three weeks ago?"

Oh, great. We get the one person on this island who thinks laws are supposed to be *obeyed*, dammit. I immediately adopt a look of stupefied ignorance, a strategy that I do quite effectively. "Gee, we were having such a lovely time here, we didn't notice."

The agent puts on her sternest expression. "You could be deported for this."

I resist pointing out the irony of being thrown out of a country for trying to leave. "Oh, we're really sorry," I plead fervently. "We're really, *really* sorry."

At this very moment, Porkchop shows up. "There you are!" He gives us a big hug. "I didn't want you to take off before I could give you this." He hands me a brown paper bag.

The agent is in no mood to be ignored. "Do you know these people?"

"Yes, they're my friends."

She shows him our passports. "Well, your friends' visas have expired."

Porkchop places a hand on her shoulder. "Just for me, could you please forgive them?"

Her face softens. "Well, just this once." She hands our passports back, her visage once again stern. "But remember not to do it next time."

We promise and then give Porkchop one last hug before he rushes off, back to the kitchen. When we get to the departure lounge, I sit down and open the bag to admire two tortillas—pork and pineapple never smelled so good.

"I can't believe it," I say to Linda. "They let us go just on the word of a cook."

Mama Manu, who is off to New Zealand to visit her sister, sits down beside us. "That's because everyone loves and respects Porkchop."

"Really?"

"Yep." Mama Manu pulls a tortilla out of the bag and takes a bite. "Doesn't hurt his pa is minister of justice, either." ■

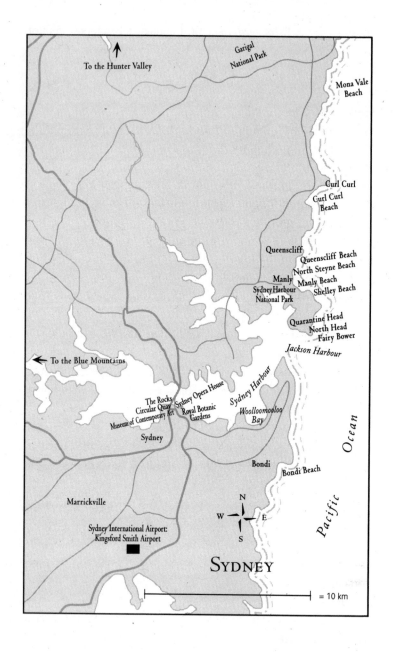

To the Hunter Valley

Garigal
National Park

Mona Vale
Beach

Curl Curl

Curl Curl
Beach

Queenscliff

Queenscliff Beach
North Steyne Beach
Manly Beach
Shelley Beach

Manly
Sydney Harbour
National Park

Quarantine Head
North Head
Fairy Bower

Jackson Harbour

To the Blue Mountains

The Rocks
Circular Quay

Museum of Contemporary Art

Sydney Opera House
Royal Botanic
Gardens

Sydney Harbour

Woolloomooloo
Bay

Sydney

Bondi

Bondi Beach

Marrickville

N
W E
S

Pacific Ocean

Sydney International Airport:
Kingsford Smith Airport

SYDNEY

Pacific

= 10 km

CHAPTER 4

Oz You Like It

As our plane arrives over Australia, the first light of day effuses the eastern edge of the continent with vibrant warmth, the thick forests that dot the indented shores taking on a reddish-green hue. The plane banks over Botany Bay and comes to rest at Sydney Airport. We disembark and present our visas to an immigration agent, a fair-haired man with a ruddy complexion. He stamps our passports and gives me a smile.

"Welcome to Oz, mate." He pronounces it *might*, right out of *Crocodile Dundee*, and I almost burst out laughing, but catch myself at the last moment. Although my sense of humour tends toward funny accents, his might incline toward latex gloves and cavity searches. I keep my mirth under wraps until we are free and clear of customs.

Sydney Airport is modern and airy and looks pretty much like any other airport in the world; my interest is in finding the CityRail station. Sydney is admirably served by a train system that runs from the airport to the centre of town, as well as to a host of suburbs spread up and down the coast. We locate the station in the international terminal, purchase our tickets, and head into town.

We rattle along for about five kilometres, our train sometimes hanging high above the rooftops of surrounding suburbs, other times disappearing into tunnels beneath expansive parks. We eventually emerge at Circular Quay, surrounded on three sides by immense office towers and brilliant blue water on the fourth. Circular Quay is the main terminus for the ferries that service the harbour. It is morning rush hour and dozens of boats are bustling in to disgorge suburbanites heading for work. We are soon outbound toward Manly.

Most North American or European tourists invariably make their way to Bondi, Sydney's most famous beach, to partake of the surfing, partying, and generic hedonistic Australian lifestyle, but we aren't especially interested in spending six months in a tourist ghetto. We want to find a place that is accessible to the attractions that Sydney has to offer, but isolated enough to have a small-town atmosphere where meeting your neighbours and experiencing life the way the locals do are still possible. We aren't just looking for a holiday—we are looking for a *home*.

Manly seems to fit our needs precisely. Although only some ten kilometres across the harbour from the centre of Sydney, less than half an hour by ferry, it developed as a unique, separate town a century ago, long before urban sprawl swallowed it up into the greater metropolis. It has its own town centre, tree-lined residential streets, and a quiet charm far from the hustle and bustle of big city life. The fact that it has a topless beach doesn't hurt, either.

To our left, as we ride the ferry toward Manly, is Sydney Bridge, an immense expanse of steel girders, stretching across to the north shore. To our right is the Sydney Opera House, a stunning, internationally recognized architectural monument. As we skim across the waves, I glance down at the clear blue waters. A school of dolphins splash along in the wake of the boat. As the pilot weaves among the sailboats that dot the bay, the dolphins easily keep abreast of our racing craft. They only drop away as we slow for the ferry terminal, no doubt bored by the slow pace.

The main wharf at Manly juts some fifty metres into the harbour; behind it squats a glass-and-aluminum mall, housing shops and restaurants. To the left is a seawater aquarium, to the right a marina in which sailboats bob in the gentle surf. We disembark and make our way toward town. Our prospective new home is situated on a high spit of sandy land, which extends from the main shore out to a hill of granite. The spit runs roughly north to south—on the west side, rests the inner harbour, on the east, the South Pacific Ocean.

Manly peninsula was a traditional hunting and fishing ground for several thousand years. When Captain Arthur Phillip met the naked locals here in 1788, he immediately commented on their "manly" physiques, and the name stuck. Unfortunately, the Aborigines were soon run off in the name of civilization, which, in this case, took the form of cotton candy. The area's first non-Aboriginal residents arrived in the 1850s, when land promoter Henry Gilbert Smith set up an amusement park and began to run day steamers from Sydney. Over the next few years, he built hotels, restaurants, and other amusements by the beach. Manly soon became a chic retreat for wealthy Sydney-siders, and the spit of land gradually filled up with resort homes. By the turn of the twentieth century, as many as thirty thousand day visitors made their way to Manly to enjoy the various distractions on the main drag, christened the Corso, after the Italian term for main street.

Over the next few decades, however, Manly slowly fell on hard times. As the beach became polluted with sewage, the day trippers drifted off to cleaner realms and the buildings on the Corso became home to disreputable bingo halls. It wasn't until the last few decades that efforts were made to revive Manly's fortunes by reducing pollution and rejuvenating the Corso. Sydney-siders, attracted by affordable housing within commuting distance of the city centre, helped to swell the permanent population to its current forty-thousand range by purchasing homes there, and it is now once again a major attraction for day trippers, as well as a much-sought-after destination for frostbitten Canadians hiding from winter.

As we walk along a side street, our carry-on bags clicking along the sidewalk behind us, various people nod and smile as we pass. The roads are wide and lined with shady trees, and the houses and commercial buildings have, for the most part, an elegance and charm to them. We stop beneath a large, shady tree and pull out our map. Captain Billy, who has stayed in Manly several times, has recommended a stay at the Dew Drop Inn. "It's cheap, close to everything I need, and clean," he said. I follow the map directions to a road running across the south side of the spit, where the spruced-up image of Manly takes a distinct turn for the sordid.

The Dew Drop Inn is, as Captain Billy promised, close to everything *he* needs. On one side is a bottle shop and, on the other side, judging from the girls lounging on its back steps, a whorehouse. Inside, the inn is laid out in monastery style: a series of Spartan cells, with the bathroom conveniently located at the end of the hall. Each room comes with a mattress, seemingly purchased from a juvenile offenders' camp, and the ceilings appear to be decorated with either grey stipple or bat dung.

"Do you think Captain Billy was drunk or stoned when he stayed here?" I ask.

"I'd go for insane," says Linda.

Fortunately, it is mid-October, still spring in Sydney, and numerous nearby hotels and inns all sport vacancy signs. They also appear to be on the delightfully seedy side. "Collar TV" advertises one, perhaps as a treat for your dog. "Rent by the Day or Week" says another; if you want to rent by the hour, try the place next to the Dew Drop Inn, I suppose.

The Budapest Hotel catches my eye. It is a series of bungalows, run together into a motel-like affair by arches of pink plaster, and with a sign offering "Try our Honeymoon Suite." Intrigued, we enter to inquire. The Budapest is owned and operated by Gabor, an East European, who has complemented his short stature and comb over by tanning his skin to a lobster hue. Gabor also has a stooped posture and a remarkable set of eyes— large, brown orbs undercut by thick, black bags, which give him the air of a basset hound awaiting a kick.

When we ask about the suite, Gabor collects a key from behind the office counter and leads us down a dim hallway. As he shuffles along, he explains in a mix of English and Hungarian that the suite is the former residence of his estranged wife, before he threw her out for trying to serve him tea laced with sink cleanser. He unlocks the door, and we enter.

The unit is divided into a small bedroom/sitting room, complete with *collar* TV and burgundy-flocked wallpaper, a kitchen that features a steel counter pinched off a fish trawler, and a bathroom in which the shower curtain bears an eerie resemblance to the lining of a coffin. Perhaps an amorous subterranean mammal might consider this a honeymoon suite, as the entire room is lit by only a tiny window, covered in iron bars. But hey, at fifty dollars a night, it will do for a week or two until we find a permanent place. We shake Gabor's hand, pay our first week's rent, and settle into what we quickly dub the Mole Hole.

Or, at least, we settle in for the first five minutes. That's how long it takes to discover that it is completely devoid of such luxuries as soap, toilet paper, and wine. Gabor reluctantly rustles up the first two items, but informs us in no uncertain terms that we are responsible for the latter. *Buggah*, as they say in Oz. We don walking shoes and venture forth.

Some ninety metres to the east, we come to South Steyne Road, at the southern end of Manly Beach. Before us, the South Pacific Ocean, aquamarine and flecked with choppy surf, stretches all the way to Chile. To our right, the road climbs a granite outcrop to a hill dotted with homes and, to our left, stretches a magnificent arc of sand, some sixty metres wide and perhaps three kilometres long. We decide the groceries can wait; it is low tide and the fine, brown sand, so soft beneath our now-naked feet, is speckled with tiny crabs. A bright-red inflatable boat, complete with outboard motor, rests in front of the Manly Life Saving Club, ready to wing off in pursuit of errant swimmers.

Not that it is needed today. We walk down to the water, dip our toes in the surf, and swiftly scurry back. The sand may feel warm, but it will obviously take a few more weeks of sun for the water to lose its Antarctic charm. Undaunted, we continue north. Since it is still spring, the beach is sparsely populated and those in attendance aren't overly enthusiastic about doffing too many clothes in light of the strong, cool breeze. We turn our attention, instead, to a row of Norfolk pines. There must be a hundred of them growing in a line along the beach. Captain Billy described them as magnificent, but I find that a trifle grand. Most of the mature specimens have lost their lower branches due to some arboreal equivalent of leprosy and now present a profile consisting of a long, slender trunk, topped by a head of spiky green. They remind me of giant toilet brushes, and as they gently sway in unison to the onshore breeze, I can't help but imagine a TV commercial for Vim cleanser.

We reach the junction of South Steyne and the famous Corso, where a flock of seagulls is gathered. Linda, who, at the age of four, was pecked in the eye by a turkey on her grandfather's farm, hates all birds with a passion. "They're nothing but shit hawks," she announces, as she tries to skirt around them. We are almost clear of the flock when an unwary woman emerges from a chip shop, carrying a tray of French fries. The large birds rise en masse and flurry about her, screeching and crashing into one another as if they're competing in an avian roller derby. The woman panics and begins to run, arms flailing, until the chips lie scattered about. The gulls immediately settle onto the ground, their feast assured. Linda points a finger at the feathery thugs: "If I had an Uzi, I'd shoot the lot of them."

The Corso, a pedestrian street stretching from the ferry marina to the beach, is about thirty metres wide, with a parade of palm trees down its middle. Retail stores, restaurants, and civic buildings, most restored to the area's heyday period of the 1930s, line each side. A pair of buildings on the right catches my attention: the Steyne and Bristol Hotels. Sitting across the street from one another, they share a colonial-style motif—long, low, wood buildings, with a covered walkway and second-storey balcony. A neon Foster's sign blinks in the upstairs window of the Bristol, and I make a mental note to come back sometime for a few pints.

We proceed down the Corso until we come to Coles, a food outlet. The air-conditioned aisles are stocked in great abundance with many of the same brands I am used to seeing in North America, something I find a bit disappointing. Perhaps it is naïve to expect to find Dingo Chow in the pet-food aisle, but I thought that, halfway around the world, I might find *something* unique, perhaps tinned kangaroo or great white shark-fin soup. I am also struck by how organized everything seems to be—cans of beans impeccably stacked, and zucchini precisely aligned in the vegetable section. Someone obviously goes to great lengths to beat any vestige of famous Oz disrespect for order out of the staff. I begin to yearn for Raro's grocery store, which seemed as if it was organized by the Marx Brothers. Sufficiently air-conditioned but slightly deflated, we traverse the aisles, picking up the kitchen and cleaning basics we need to get the Mole Hole in proper subterranean order.

After passing through the checkout, we exit back onto the Corso to enter the adjacent liquor store, also owned by Coles. Thanks to the Victorian-era aversion to, *horrors*, drinking alcohol-laced beverages with meals, the powers-that-be decreed that the liquor and food departments in every supermarket must be physically separated by a two-metre-high wall running down the middle of the store. As I enter the bottle shop, I idly entertain the idea of conspiring with a confederate on the grocery side to chuck a bottle of pickles over the wall into my waiting hands, when I am distracted by an immense yellow sign with the most beautiful sentence in the English language: "Buy a dozen, get 10% off." No words penned by Shakespeare have ever moved me more. In the time it takes to shake a wallaby's tail, I round up my selection and cart it to the till.

Only one problem remains: getting it home. We are perhaps half a kilometre from the Mole Hole, and I'll be damned if I'm going to waste the cost of a pint on a cab. I have standards, you know. We have no choice but to split up my purchase into four bags of three, then hoof it back. By the time we arrive, my arms are sufficiently extended that I can reach from the couch in the sitting room to the cupboard drawers on the far wall. Mind you, it makes it easy to fetch the corkscrew.

The following Saturday, I decide it's time to locate my old mate Greg Painter. I first met the native Sydney-sider on the island of Koh Samui, some ten years before, while touring the southern part of Thailand on an extended wanderlust. Unlike the Australian stereotype of beer-swilling yobs, Greg maintained an intelligent, cultivated air, primarily through the laudable habit of keeping his mouth shut and ears open. We became immediate friends, and some years later, he stayed with me in Calgary, before we journeyed south to Mexico for a fine winter of tequila and undocumented adventures.

One propensity that Greg does share with most Australians is his love of extended travel, eschewing a permanent job and residence in order to save sufficient funds to journey from Borneo to Monaco. Unfortunately, this has made it rather hard to keep track of him, and I have no idea where he might be living in Sydney or even if he is currently on this side of the planet, as I haven't heard from him in several years.

Fortunately, I possess an investigative ability honed by years of interrogating city councillors and varied public relations minions. Using a technique I actually learned from reading Mickey Spillane novels, I gather a small stack of coins and head to the nearest phone booth, where I begin to systematically call the dozen *Painters, G.*, listed in the phone book. The first two do not answer, the third is a George Painter, the fourth, a Gwyneth. The fifth, an elderly gentleman a tad hard of hearing, simply says, no, he doesn't want his house painted. My stack of coins has dwindled, and I only have enough for one more call, so I plunk it down and spin the dial. A man answers and I can tell it isn't my friend, but I decide to ask anyway. "Could I speak to Greg?"

"Sure, hold on a moment." I can hear someone walking away from the phone, then shouting into the distance. "It's for you!"

A few moments later, Greg picks up the phone. "Hello?"

"Greg, it's Gord. How are you?"

"Wonderful! Where are you?"

"I'm in Manly. Linda and I got here just a few days ago."

"What are you doing today?"

"Not a lot, how about you?"

"I'm getting married. Would you like to come?"

Linda is sitting on the motel patio, reading the morning paper, when I burst in. "Hurry up, we have to get dressed. We're going to Greg's wedding!"

Linda looks up in surprise and delight. "Who's he getting married to?"

"A girl, I think." I *shoosh* her toward the Mole Hole. "Hurry, the ceremony starts in half an hour."

Linda is ready in ten minutes. We hasten outside, hail a cab, and hop into the back seat. The driver is a rather likeable chap from the Indian Subcontinent. The licence over the dash says his name is Raj. "We're on our way to a wedding, you have to hurry," I tell him.

"Very good," he says. "I love weddings."

I pull out a slip of paper with the address of the ceremony and hand it to him. "Do you know where Carisbrook House is? It's a historic museum or something."

"Oh yes, yes, of course." Raj shifts into gear and we barrel away in a squeal of rubber. "I will have you there in a jiffy."

We are soon on a main road, racing west. Fortunately, the Saturday morning traffic is fairly light, and we seem to be making good headway. After a few minutes, however, I notice that Raj seems to be distracted downward, to something inside the car. Curious, I peek into the front seat and spy him fiddling with a detailed map book that shows all the addresses in the city. "You don't know where Carisbrook House is, do you?"

Raj smiles sheepishly. "I think it is in Lane Cove, no?"

I haven't a bloody clue, but I'm not about to waste time. I grab the book and open it to the index. "You drive and I'll direct."

By good fortune, Raj has made an excellent start in the right direction, and we follow a major road to the heart of Lane Cove, a suburb northwest of Sydney proper. Carisbrook House is located a few blocks toward the bay, and we arrive with minutes to spare.

The house, built by affluent settlers, is a nineteenth-century, Victorian-style stone cottage, set on a large, landscaped estate that flows down the hill to the mouth of the Lane Cove River. Greg is standing out front, dressed in a black wool, double-breasted suit. Even though it is his wedding day, and thirty-five degrees Celsius in the shade, he is looking cool and composed. He gives me a big hug and pats me on the stomach. "My, my, somebody's put on a little weight, haven't they?"

Greg is about to be married to Heather, a fitness instructor. Greg, who has never in the past exhibited interest in any sport more strenuous than opening a beer bottle, has developed a penchant for cycling and running great distances in the blistering heat. He looks very svelte and toned in his double-breasted suit and reminds me of a movie star—sort of a tall James Cagney, with puffy eyes. I tell the groom he looks very handsome and introduce him to Linda, whom he has never met. We are, in turn, introduced to his best man, Alex.

Our conversation is interrupted by the arrival of the bride. Heather, a slim, pretty blonde, is dressed in an elegant white gown and carrying a bouquet of white roses. Greg takes her by the arm and escorts her down a garden path to a shaded copse behind the house, where several dozen friends and family are gathered to witness the ceremony.

The couple is flanked by best man Alex and Heather's maid of honour, Jenny. The minister conducts a moving ceremony, and perhaps it is the heat, or maybe some exotic pollen in the air, but I find myself beginning to blubber. Fortunately, a small, noisy ground bird breaks cover from beneath a rhododendron and squawks in indignation at the interlopers in its grove, creating a sufficient distraction for me to blow my nose. Greg and Heather exchange rings and kiss, then we all retire to a reception behind the house.

With the nuptials over, we get a chance to catch up on all the news. Greg has been working as a courier in Sydney for the last few years; he has given up his perennial travels for the sake of marital bliss. He and Heather own a home in Marrickville, a rather rough-but-colourful section of town. "We have a puppy named Poppy, but we plan to start a family soon," explains Heather. I learn that it is doubly fortunate I contacted them this morning, as they are on their way, directly from the wedding, to Bali for an extended honeymoon.

When Greg and Heather are called away to sign their wedding documents, Linda and I take the opportunity to introduce ourselves more fully to the best man, Alex, and to Alex's wife, Jenny, Heather's maid of honour. Alex, whom Greg has known since grade school, is tall and broad shouldered, with a dark complexion and black, curly hair. "We were just on our way out the door when you called," he explains. "The only reason we answered the phone was because we were running a little late and thought they were calling us to see what the holdup was." Fate is like that sometimes, isn't it? Jenny is pale, with dark brown hair, and much shorter than Alex. They are teachers, have two small children, and live near the Garigal, a national forest that borders the northern reaches of Sydney. They promise to invite us to their home for shrimp on the barbie and other local delights.

Greg returns briefly to say goodbye; the limousine is waiting to take them to the airport. "Just make sure you don't use an outhouse while I'm gone," he says.

This is the sort of comment that makes my bowels shiver. "Why, what's in an outhouse?"

"Oh, just outhouse spiders. They make a little funnel-shaped lair under the seat, and when you sit down, they leap up and bite your *goolies*."

I'm not sure what goolies are, but I suspect I have a pair that takes poorly to spider bites. "Is it painful?"

"Not for long." The limo pulls up, and Greg goes to fetch Heather. "You're usually dead before you can pull your pants up."

Well, that's a blessing.

"What are you staring at?"

It is early morning, a few days after Greg and Heather's wedding, and Linda has caught me standing in front of the bathroom's full-length mirror, dressed in nothing but shorts and my bunny slippers. "Do you think I'm fat?" I ask.

Linda is eating a bowl of yoghurt. She has made it a personal goal to lose ten pounds on our travels and tends to favour such dubious fare as fruit and vegetables, over what I consider far more-nutritive staples such as corn dogs and pickled eggs. "No, I'd say you're no more than puffy."

Oh, that's reassuring. Okay, I know I'm not really svelte—I've always had a fondness for stale newsroom doughnuts—but Greg's comment about being chubby bugs me. If I'm going to lounge about on a topless beach all day, then I'll have to do something about the spare tire. Linda has never had a problem with keeping slim and enjoys aerobics so much, she actually teaches it. I, on the other hand, would rather give manicures to crocodiles than wrap my butt in Lycra and do ab crunches to ABBA. I need a way to lose weight that is effortless and requires no special coordination or ability.

"Why don't you take up running?" suggests Linda.

"You have to be crazy to run."

"See—you have what it takes."

I take that as a compliment. "What about injuries? Don't you get runner's elbow, or something?"

"You're thinking of shin splints. And you don't get them if you wear proper shoes."

"What if I spend money on shoes and find out I'm no good at it?"

Linda thinks for a moment. "I have an idea. Why don't you start on the sand? You can run barefoot, no problem. That way, you can see if you like it. I'll even join you."

Having run out of excuses, I reluctantly agree. We dress in shorts and T-shirts and set off for the beach. It is a beautiful day, not a cloud in the sky. Even though it's only around 9:00 AM, the sun is warm enough to stifle the chill of the onshore breeze.

Beach volleyball is a popular sport in Manly, and the beach is bustling with workers setting up tents, bleachers, and nets for a tournament later in the week. We do a series of stretches, then set off at an energetic pace along the shore. At first, I feel somewhat awkward, trying to find the right stride, but after a few hundred metres, I find a comfortable gait and actually begin to enjoy myself. It's a wonderful feeling, pounding along the firm sand that rims the water, the sea breeze in your hair and the sight of two young women in very tiny thongs collecting rays. I am almost past them before I realize that I have spotted my very first topless birds of the season. I swivel my head in a totally involuntary, hetero-sexual reflex and barrel headlong into a tent guy wire, stubbing my toe on the cement anchor and cartwheeling into the sand.

Linda stares back at the girls. "That's it, no more running on the sand for you."

My toe is turning a pleasant shade of purple. "I can't run on the cement in bare feet, it's too hard."

"In that case, we're going to have to buy you some shoes."

And that is why we find ourselves on the harbour ferry the next day, heading into central Sydney. After landing at Circular

Quay, we head south along Pitt Street for several hundred metres until the office towers give way to shops, cinemas, and restaurants. About a kilometre south of the harbour, we come to a pedestrian mall. After the concrete canyon surrounding Circular Quay, I find the mall's statues, fountains, and wide sidewalks much preferable, although I will say that Sydney-siders have a rather unnerving habit of striding right at you, then breaking off at the very last moment. I start to yearn for a cattle prod.

The Strand Arcade is a retail laneway, about fifteen metres wide and perhaps ninety metres long. Shops line both sides to a height of three storeys. The entire mall is capped by a graceful ironwork-and-glass roof, some eighteen metres above ground level. Large baskets of ferns and flowers hang from wires along its entire length, basking in the natural light. An odd perfume, half-lucre and half-gardenia, hangs in the air.

The store we're looking for, Shoes R' Oz, is on the third floor. We accidentally go up the wrong side of the mall before we spot it, but fortunately, a glass walkway spans both sides. On the walkway, a mime is drinking an imaginary bottle of beer and winks and rubs his stomach in appreciation as we pass. I idly wonder if he is packing an imaginary parachute, but Linda, reading my mind, grabs me by the arm and pulls me into the store.

The store contains every imaginable combination of sports shoe, from basketball trainers to ironman triathlon slippers. Derek, our clerk, is pimply, affable, and more than willing to help. He peers closely at my current shoe and deduces that I have a slightly supinated gait, which is a polite way of saying I'm pigeon-toed. He pulls down a pair of sparkly blue-and-white shoes. "This is the Cosmic 3000," he explains. "You'll go a blue streak, mate."

I lace them up and take a few tentative strides around the aisle. They feel fine, but I note that the laces have come undone. I squat and use the double-knot technique taught to me by Miss Grundy in first grade, but by the time I return to

Derek, they have come undone again.

"What's with the laces?" I ask.

"Oh, those are the new DynaKevlah brand," he explains. "They're bulletproof, bioluminescent, and so strong you can pick up a combi-van with the suckers."

"But they won't stay tied."

"Yeah," he concedes. "They're crap at that."

By the time we return to Manly, it is too hot to run, even along the shady portion of the promenade beneath the giant Norfolk pines, and we retire to the Budapest Hotel. Linda goes into the Mole Hole to prepare dinner, and I go out onto the hotel patio to see if there is a free table. Gabor has turned the inner courtyard into a rather comfortable retreat, with a shady, vine-covered arbour, lounge chairs and tables, and a trampoline for his kids to risk spinal paralysis on.

Gabor has also installed a large gas barbecue. Two young men, dressed in khaki shorts and blue shirts, with button-down epaulets on the shoulders, are stationed in front of the grill. Both are very large, well over six feet tall, and the pint cans of Foster's gripped in their hands look like fruit-cocktail shooters. They are turning wieners on the grill, which, as soon as one is sufficiently charred, they spear with a fork, dunk in a jar of mustard, and eat like a dill pickle. I have seen them in passing once or twice over the last week, but have never had a chance to talk to them until now.

I compliment their bachelor skills, and they introduce themselves as Bruce and Bruce, here in Sydney from the northern town of Cairns to qualify as river pilots.

"How do you like Sydney?" I ask.

"It's *rippah*," says Bruce One.

Bruce Two holds up a black wiener. "Care for a bite? They're *rippah*."

I politely decline. "What's it like being a river pilot in Cairns?"

"It's *rippah*," says Bruce One.

"You gotta watch out for the sandbars," says Bruce Two.

"And the saltwater crocs, of course," adds Bruce One. They both nod in unison. "*They're* rippah."

I go back to the Mole Hole, where Linda is examining a bag of zucchini for survivors, the fridge having decided to freeze them into mush. "I just ran into Bruce and Bruce," I say. "They're very odd."

"Yeah, I know. I met them this morning."

"Do you think they got that way from staying here?"

"What do you think?" ·

"I think it's time to find a new place."

Linda chucks the zucchini into the garbage. "*Rippah*." ∎

CHAPTER 5

A Room with a Cockroach

By now, it is early November, and having definitely taken a shine to Manly, we decide to stay for the next several months. On Gabor's advice, we head for a real estate agency, which is not as odd as it sounds. In Australia, realtors are largely based in neighbourhoods and work out of storefront offices, posting both sales and rental notices in the window. Gabor has recommended the firm of John Redding & Son, located near the Corso. We glance at the notices in its window, and since there are a fair number of rentals in our price range, we enter.

The front office is deserted, but the bell that rings over the doorway soon summons Elizabeth, a matronly woman in a summer floral-print dress and cat's-eye glasses; she has powdered her face and applied blush. When we explain we are looking for a rental property, she picks up a phone at the reception desk and pushes a button. "There's a lovely couple looking for a rental," she says. "Right, I'll tell them you'll be down in a sec." She directs us to a loveseat, where we sit examining a binder with notices for various properties until the real estate agent arrives from upstairs.

John Redding, who is in his late fifties or early sixties, wears a grey wool suit and a blue silk tie, spotted with what appears to be marinara sauce. He has thick, black glasses, jowls that spill over his shirt collar, and the hairiest pair of eyebrows I have ever seen on a primate walking upright.

We introduce ourselves and explain that we'd like to rent a

furnished apartment in Manly. His eyebrows arch skyward, and he looks at us as if this is a most unusual request. "Do you have references?" he asks.

Having been warned before we left Canada that this is normal practice in Sydney, I pull out several letters from our lawyer, banker, and accountant. Redding takes them and examines each one carefully. "Calgary, eh?" he says. He pulls a rather beaten atlas out of the reception desk and flips through it until he finds the map of Canada. Peering closely at the map, he soon finds the relevant city and, alternating between the map and the letters, confirms that the spellings do indeed match. Having verified our references, he slams the atlas shut and straightens up. "Right. What price range do we have in mind?"

I hold up several notices, taken from his binder, in the range of $550 per month, which is about $600 in Australian dollars. Redding takes the notices and studies them. "Humph, yes, comfortable residences all. I shall have my number one assistant show you around." He nods to Elizabeth, who once again dials the phone.

"Malcolm, love, can you come down? We have someone here for a rental tour."

Malcolm, who is the Reddings' son, descends the stairs three at a time, while knotting his tie. He is perhaps twenty-one and has the physique of a rugby player, the collar on his shirt being about ten centimetres short of completing the gap. He shakes our hands, grabs a mitt full of keys, and rushes us out the door. Keeping up with Malcolm is a bit of a challenge, but worth the effort when crossing streets. Cars and lorries tend to screech to a halt when he launches himself out into the road, no doubt fearing serious trauma to the bodywork in the event of impact.

The first rental unit we see is a charming walkup behind a Chinese takeaway. Not only are the walls cracked in that authentic heritage manner, but the odour emanating from the restaurant's garbage bin is evocative of exotic locales, in this case, a Malaysian ditch. We pass. The second place is a small bungalow on a busy street, artfully situated so that the dust kicked up by passing buses blows invitingly through the front door. The interior's peeling walls and other decorative touches make me suspect the owner is just waiting for it to be rezoned as a burger joint. "Is this all that's available for six hundred a month?" I ask.

Malcolm nods. "Pretty much."

"Is there anything by the beach?" asks Linda. "We'd really like to be able to look out over the ocean."

Malcolm rubs his chin. "I *do* have a furnished one bedroom, but it's a bit more pricey."

"Is it clean?" asks Linda.

"Yeah, it's in great nick. Just redone, too."

"Let's have a look then," I say.

Malcolm leads us down a side street until we reach North Steyne Road. As promised, the Seaview directly overlooks the beach. A cement high-rise from the East European Academy of Architecture and Tractor Design, its exterior is painted in the kinds of light blue and purple hues that make you wish colour blindness tests were mandatory for landlords. But, otherwise, it looks like it is in good repair, and we decide to go up and have a look. We accompany Malcolm in the elevator to the fifth floor.

The one-bedroom unit is rather small, no more than forty square metres, but it is bright and airy. Malcolm finds a pile of surf-fishing magazines on the coffee table and immerses himself in them, while we scout out the unit. The walls have indeed been recently repainted and the carpet replaced. The beige-dull furniture is modern, but service-able. The kicker, however, is the balcony. Even though the apartment is on the side of the building that faces away from the ocean, the balcony juts out far enough to afford a good view of the beach and the water beyond. "How much is it?" asks Linda.

Malcolm, his nose inserted deeply into a barracuda, doesn't even glance up. "A thousand a month, everything included."

I do a quick mental conversion—that's about nine hundred

Canadian dollars. "How long would it take to move in?"

Malcolm tucks the magazines under his arm. "Assuming there's no problem with the paperwork or clearing your deposit, how does Monday sound?"

I shake his hand. "It sounds like a deal."

The next several days are a scramble of phone calls to our banker in Canada and forms to complete. On the appointed day, we load our meagre belongings into a red Radio Flyer pull wagon supplied by Gabor's son and wheel our way down South Steyne to our new home. I cannot begin to describe the conflicting emotions that run through my breast—the joy of leaving the Mole Hole, the excitement of actually living for a whole winter without snow, the embarrassment of pulling a child's toy down a major roadway—but the feeling lasts for as long as it takes to unlock the door, dump our possessions in the middle of the room, and get a good look at the wall art. Linda points to an oil painting hanging over the phone table that she hadn't noticed before. "What *is* that?"

I move closer for a better look. It is a large swirl of orange and brown, which I originally mistook for an abstract study. On closer inspection, however, it turns out to depict a raging forest fire, consuming a bush shack. Worst of all, it is apparently screwed to the wall, no doubt to prevent it from being tossed off the balcony. I shrug. "Maybe we can put something over it."

"How about plaster?" Linda picks up our luggage and takes it into the bedroom to put away, while I unload our assortment of utensils and foodstuffs salvaged from the Mole Hole. I then return to the living room to test out the furniture, two chairs and a loveseat, all upholstered in matching tufted fabric of synthetic provenance. The loveseat sags beneath my weight in a genial way, providing a cocoon-like indent, but a waft of something that reminds me of a morgue assaults my nostrils. As I lift a cushion to inspect for remnants of a previous tenant, I am interrupted by a scream from the bedroom. I rush in to find Linda staring at the floor and pointing a broom in the general direction of the bed.

"What's wrong?" I ask.

"It flew in through the window and crawled under the bed!"

"What, a vampire?"

"No, a cockroach!"

"A *cockroach*?" I slap my forehead. "I thought it was something terrible. You scared the crap out of me."

Linda keeps her stare focused on the bed, the broom still in attack mode. "It's a *big* cockroach."

"Yeah, right." I swagger in manly fashion to the bed, bend over, and lift the bed cover, then leap back. It is, without a doubt, the biggest, ugliest cockroach I have ever seen outside a Japanese monster movie. I take Linda by the arm, back out of the room, and close the door.

"What are you doing?" she asks.

"Maybe it will just take my wallet and leave."

Linda pokes me in the chest. "If you don't get that insect out from under the bed, then I'm not sleeping in there tonight, *got it*?"

Got it. I get some oven mitts from the kitchen, grip the broom in my hands, take a deep breath, and open the bedroom door. Linda pushes me through, then closes the door behind me.

I stand perfectly still, scanning the room. As far as I can tell, it is still under the bed. Lifting the cover with the end of the broom, I glance under. It glares back at me, wiggling its antennae in menacing fashion. I suddenly have an inspiration. I open the window wide, then go back to the far side of the bed and push the broom toward the cockroach, urging it forward. Sure enough, the insect crawls out from under the bed, spreads its wings, and takes to the air with a *clicky-whirling* noise. I grab a pillow, in case it launches a counterattack, and use the broom to guide it toward the window, where it zooms out without further ado. I make several thrashing noises and then slam the window shut. I open the door and step proudly into the living room.

"Have no fear, my dear, he won't ever bother you again."

"My hero." Linda looks deeply into my eyes and hands me a toilet brush. "The bathroom needs cleaning."

By early evening, we have most of our new home cleaned and sorted, and we retire to the balcony to celebrate with a bottle of Oz bubbly. Our choice of libation is named, appropriately enough, Seaview, and as we pour our first glass, the moon rises from the ocean, big and silvery and shiny.

"Here's to our new home," I toast, lifting my glass aloft.

Linda points out to sea, to the right of the moon. "Look, it's the *Queen Elizabeth*!"

The luxury ocean liner, on an extended cruise of the South Seas, is leaving Sydney Harbour on its way to Bali. Its lights twinkle as it crosses the silvery wake of the moon. I am suddenly struck by the fact that I am standing looking down on a moonlit beach, with the woman I love in my arms, sipping a cold glass of bubbly, and I am filled with a light, almost giddy sense of happiness. It is a perfect moment, and I savour it long after the *QE II* is lost from view.

Alas, the moment ends—they must be making the hole in the top of bubbly bottles larger these days because, in no time at all, the bottle is empty. We decide the decent thing to do now is to go for a walk on the beach. The surf is a sparkling, foamy white in the moonlight, as we run barefoot through the sand, cutting into the water to kick sprays of water over each other. By the time we reach the Corso, we are thoroughly soaked. Fortunately, the few bills I have stuffed in my pocket are unaffected by the sea water, and we decide it is the perfect time for a pint.

The Bristol Hotel is not nearly as grand as the Steyne, but I notice that the tiny balconies atop the second floor are largely deserted and would make an excellent perch to watch the world go by and get ourselves dry. We enter the hotel and ascend the stairs to the second floor, which consists largely of a sports bar, equipped with a pool table and several TV sets turned to rugby. I order two pints of Foster's from the barmaid, who accepts my soggy fiver with hardly a glance. We exit through a set of balcony doors and sit down at a tiny wrought-iron table. Beneath our feet, the Corso is filled with late-night strollers out for some refreshing cool air. We clink our glasses and admire the scene.

For about thirty seconds, that is. I am idly glancing toward a palm tree when I notice what I had first taken to be a coconut is spreading out a pair of thin, spidery wings about a metre across. Dropping from its upside-down perch, the creature begins to flop through the air, directly toward our beer. We duck as it sails by just above our heads, before angling back toward the Corso and drifting off into the night. We grab our drinks and run back into the bar. "What was that?" I shout at the barmaid.

"What?"

"That big Dracula thing."

"Oh, that's a fruit bat. Harmless. They come into town now and again from the forests north of Sydney."

That's what I love about this country. It's got bouncing marsupials, leaping poisonous spiders, and monster cockroaches galore, but there's always room for one more beer-sucking bat.

The next day, I discover one of the Seaview's finest amenities: its clothesline. The line is actually a rotating device made of aluminum, sort of like an upside-down umbrella with no skin. A series of lines, stretched between the tines, allows you to attach clothing, by means of plastic pegs. All in all, it's rather pedestrian, but the unique and charming aspect of this clothesline is that it is on the roof. Standing there with dripping undies, I can scan 360 degrees, from the ocean to my east, the forested Sydney Harbour Nature Park to the south, bustling Manly to the west, and Curl Curl Beach far to the north.

It is to the north that I espy an amazing sight—a group of surfers plying the waves some ninety metres from shore at the north end of

Manly Beach. A small but virulent thunderstorm has arrived unbidden over Queenscliff Hill and is bearing down upon them, striking the water with frequent bursts of lightning. The surfers play on, seemingly unconcerned by the threat to their lives. As I finish placing wet clothing onto a metal pole atop a tall building, I can't help but wonder what kind of idiot would expose himself to that kind of danger.

I head back down and emerge onto our floor just as our neighbour Gertrude steps out from her apartment. She is about seventy-five, with frosted blue hair, creamy white skin, and pale blue eyes. Gertrude is a widow, her husband, Dennis, having passed away some ten years ago. Rather than live with her son Kevin in the suburbs, she has chosen to stay in Manly, where she can walk across the street to the beach, with her folding chair and knitting. Today, she is wearing a pale blue dress, white-lace ankle socks, and red-leather, high-heeled sandals and is carrying a racing form tucked under one arm. "What do you think you're doing?" she says.

I glance down at the hamper I'm carrying. "Laundry?"

She shakes her head. "No time for that now. Come on, we have to get going before it starts."

"Before *what* starts?"

She waves the racing sheet at me. "The Melbourne Cup, of course. I'll hold the elevator while you get your wife."

I dutifully enter our apartment and find Linda in the kitchen. "We're going out."

"Where to?"

"Melbourne, I think."

As it turns out, we're not going quite that far today—merely around the corner to the Off-Track Betting Shop. The shop is above a liquor outlet, which I always find helpful; after all, what better emollient to common sense is there than a quart of rye? Gertrude, however, eschews the bottle shop for the moment and urgently shoos us upstairs to join the queue of people waiting to place their bets.

As we stand in line, Gertrude scans her sheet. "Who do you favour?" I ask.

"I like Frisky Lad. He always runs in red and green silks—those are my favourite colours." She reads further. "But Oyster Ears wears yellow and purple—I love petunias."

Linda peers over Gertrude's shoulder. "Do any of them have 'thirteen' in their name? That's my lucky number."

Gertrude looks. "No, but Oyster Ears is listed as the thirteenth competitor. He's at twenty-five to one."

"Great. Let's go with him."

I shake my head. "I can't believe you two are picking a horse based on numerology." I take the sheet and have a glance. "Here's Danny Boy. It says he's good in the mud. Is it raining in Melbourne today?"

Gertrude glances at the track conditions posted on a chalkboard above the bookies. "Not a drop. Dry as a bone."

I read on. "Okay, here's Tasty Vittles. Says he's good in the stretch when conditions are dry. I'll go with him."

We place our bets, then head around the corner to the Duke of Wellington Pub. The Duke is the quintessential Oz bar, a dark, dingy joint, redolent of Foster's and wet cigarette butts. We find a table near the big-screen TV and order beer and the house specialty, "Succulent Steak on a Bun." The waitress returns shortly with what is, without a doubt, the chewiest piece of gristle I have ever encountered. When the knife proves hopelessly inadequate for the task, I put down the utensils, pick up the meat with my hands, and attempt to gnaw it with my incisors, to no avail.

"It's rather ironic calling *this* succulent," I complain.

"Not really," says Gertrude. "He was the slowest horse in last year's race." I am about to spit out my mouthful when I catch Gertrude winking at Linda. Really, older people have such odd senses of humour.

It's fortunate that we got to the Duke early, because the bar soon fills up. "The whole country comes to a stop for the Melbourne Cup," explains Gertrude. "It's a national tradition." The crowd has a certain nervous energy, which permeates the room. A fat, tanned bloke, with his shirt open to reveal several gold chains around his neck, is clutching a platinum blonde in a low-cut lamé dress in one arm and a large pitcher of beer in the other. Several biker types, with leather vests and Kaiser helmets, are arm-wrestling on a wobbly table, as their gals cheer them on. A couple of pensioners are laughing so hard I'm waiting for their teeth to fly across the room.

As the preliminary races finish and the big purse nears, the noise level and rowdiness builds even further, to the point where the joint is really churning. As each entrant in the Cup is led out, the spectators cheer and boo in lusty fashion. When the horses are finally lined up in their gate and the announcer shouts, "They're off!" the throng surges to their feet as one, cheering on favourites, waving their drinks in the air, and hollering a blue streak.

As the closely knit pack rounds the last turn into the stretch, my horse is in the lead by half a length. "Come on Tasty Vittles!" I shout. The words are hardly out of my mouth when a curtain of torrential rain comes down on the race, inundating the track. My horse disappears into a giant quagmire. The others surge ahead, the jockeys scoring their flanks with riding crops to urge them on.

"It's Danny Boy and Oyster Ears neck and neck," says the announcer. "Now, it's Danny Boy, now it's Oyster Ears ... it's Oyster Ears, by a nose!"

The crowd cheers and groans in equal measure, as tickets are torn and hurled in the air or kissed and clutched to breasts. Gertrude and Linda dance arm in arm, waving their betting stubs in the air. I sit and stare at the TV, the entire track now obscured by the downpour. For all I know, my nag may still be out there. I guess next year the house special will be Tasty Vittles on a Bun.

I am an observant person by nature, and my subject of scrutiny one fine Tuesday morning is Australian women—and what finer place to do it than at the beach? Since my running fiasco, I have forsaken the mobile form of observation for something more supine, in other words, a beach mat. By first *scooshing* the sand around and then laying the mat down, I form a rudimentary lounge chair. With a cool, refreshing malt beverage on my left and a bottle of protective sunscreen on my right, I prop my newspaper in front of me and peer over the top in the same spirit as James Stewart in *Rear Window*.

The daily migration begins around 10:00 AM. They arrive by ferry and travel in a northerly direction until they reach Queenscliff Beach, a popular swimming and surfing section of Manly. Australian women seem to come in two varieties: gorgeous and stunning. The gorgeous ones are generally tall, tanned, lithe, and graceful; the stunning ones are all of the above, and they also smile. Imagine Nicole Kidman or Elle Macpherson, but without any tops on, and you get the general drift.

After fifteen minutes or so of observation, I reach the point where I definitely need to cool off. Doffing my sunglasses and Panama hat, I head for the surf. During the day, the beach is continuously manned by lifeguards, who scan the water for sharks and floundering swimmers. In addition, they go out every morning and mark the riptides. Riptides form on any beach with a moderate surf, because, naturally, as the water comes in, it has to go back out. But, instead of receding in a broad plain, the water scoots sideways into relatively narrow aqueous channels and departs at high speed, which means that unwary swimmers nabbed in a riptide can suddenly find themselves hundreds of metres offshore in a matter of seconds. Those pictures of brave lifeguards, in rubber caps, leaping into their boat and crashing through the surf are usually in pursuit of a rip-*nabbee*.

Several years ago, in Thailand, Greg taught me how to spot a riptide. "Watch the waves as they come in and break," he explained. "The spot where there's no white foam on top is where the ripper's going out." The seas are relatively high today and, sure enough, several riptides have formed. The lifeguards have already plunked their flag markers along the shore, and anyone who ignores them receives an impolite reminder (via bullhorn) to get out of the water.

I advance to the approved bathing spot and wade in. The sea has warmed up sufficiently in the last few weeks to where it is now a more-comfortable twenty degrees Celsius. The water is shallow, and I paddle out fifty metres or so and position myself for bodysurfing. Bodysurfing is like regular surfing, only *you* are the board. Ideally, you stand in the shallow surf until a large wave, generally every seventh one, comes along. As it approaches, you start to stroke toward shore. The wave then lifts you along, and you skim the fifty metres in a matter of seconds, pulling out at the last moment, before the wave pounds ashore.

That's the theory. In practice, the wave usually picks me up, smashes me face first into the sandy bottom, and pinches my bathing trunks. I am then forced to squat in the surf until either my trunks wash back in my direction or some charitable soul retrieves them for me. In fact, it is precisely when I am waiting for someone to retrieve my briefs that I notice the most enchanting sea creature come bobbing by. It is an iridescent blue jellyfish, the size of a golf ball, trailing a black thread. For a moment, I forget my predicament as it drifts by, until a woman standing nearby starts to scream. She scrambles out of the water and lies on the beach, writhing. A lifeguard runs over, examines her, then stands up and blows his whistle. "Everybody out of the water," he shouts. "*Bluebottles!*"

I am filled with panic. What sort of horrible creature is this? I imagine a horde of voracious blue piranhas and cup my hands protectively over my naughty bits. Soon, I am the only person left in the water. "Come on," shouts the lifeguard. I point to my shorts bobbing in the surf, and he snatches them up and reluctantly wades in to bring them to me. As I hastily pull them on, I ask what a bluebottle is. The lifeguard points to the dainty little jellyfish. "There's one right there."

"*That's* what everybody is worried about?"

"Yeah. One of those tendrils touches you, mate, and you'll know why."

By the time we get out of the water, a second lifeguard has reached the woman. A nasty line of red welts trails across the back of her leg. The lifeguard hoists a squeeze bottle of yellow fluid and squirts some onto the woman's sores. The effect is immediate; the swelling begins to recede, and her expression of pain diminishes. "Wow, that's great," I say. "What's in the bottle?"

"Urine," explains the lifeguard. "Best thing for a bluebottle sting."

I return to my lounge chair, but a commotion of a different sort soon interrupts my repose. A group of Asian men, with a large TV camera, has arrived at the beach and begins filming the titillating goings-on. Most women simply cover up as they come near, but one woman is asleep and unaware of their presence, until the interviewer pokes a microphone near her face and asks her what it's like to be a shameless, exhibitionist hussy. She wakes up, startled at their sudden presence, and shouts one word: "George!"

A surfer the size of Whistler Mountain comes ashore. He grabs the TV camera and the cameraman clinging to it like a limpet, and he hurls both into the surf. The interviewer scurries into the water and pulls out his cohort, still attached to the camera, before the camera floats to Sri Lanka. George shakes his fist at them and they scurry off, much to the amusement of those observing.

I go back to the apartment to tell Linda about my adventures. "They had to evacuate the water because of bluebottles and then this big surfer dude threw a bunch of perverts into the water."

Linda looks at the towel wrapped around my waist. "Did you lose your bathing suit again?"

"Yeah, but a lifeguard brought it back."

"Good. I don't want you making a spectacle of yourself."

I consider this good advice and change into shorts and a T-shirt before we head out toward the Corso to find a new place for lunch. Although I consider myself a good cook, half the delight in experiencing a new country is discovering the local cuisine. Even in Australia, a place that doesn't have a native repertoire markedly different from North America's, fresh local ingredients can create savory variations in the most pedestrian of foods.

Today when we turn the corner onto the Corso, we discover an amazing transformation has taken place—a line of large, ungainly trees have burst into bloom. Decorated with immense numbers of large, lilac flowers, whose petals cover the paving stones of the pedestrian walk like a thick purple carpet, they are jacaranda trees, imported originally from South America. "They do this every spring," explains a newsagent, when I stop to inquire. "A bloody mess, if you ask me." For a moment, I am taken aback by his remark. How could something so beautiful be seen as a mess? But then, I stop to consider how happily he might react to his first sight of a foot of snow carpeting Calgary—as everyone else bends over the shovels and curses the stuff.

After a bit of snooping about the Corso, we discover, just off the main drag, an establishment with a signboard in front advertising a genuine Down Under burger, with home-ground beef, beet slices, and a fried egg topper. The interior of the café is decorated in traditional rec-room fashion, with cheap wood panelling, a dartboard, rickety wooden tables, and a couch that may have seen service on the *Lusitania*. It is also completely deserted. We sit down and, about fifteen minutes later, our waitress saunters out from the bowels of the café. She is dressed in black Doc Martens and a black mini dress, her nails painted black and her straight black hair cut in a fashion made popular by Morticia in *The Addams Family*. I expect her to melt in the midday sun at any moment.

We order the advertised house special and browse through a selection of tattoo magazines until our lunch arrives. The Down Under burger is just as good as its Raro cousin and comes with even more toppings. Unfortunately, this includes a long, black hair, which gets stuck in the gap between my front teeth and is drawn out of the hamburger patty as I stretch my arms to their full limit. Taking the offending fibre in my fingers, I call the waitress over. "Excuse me, there's a hair in my burger."

"That's impossible."

I offer exhibit A. "I believe this is one of yours."

"That's not mine."

I stare at the long, black hair on her head and back at the greasy, mustardy thread. "Oh, I think it is."

She leans toward me and clicks her black nails on the top of the table, like a skull rattling its teeth. "Are you calling me a *liar*? You know what I do to people who call me a *liar*?" My guess is she turns them into flying monkeys, but we don't stick around to find out. We put down our burgers and depart, before she can fetch her eye of newt. Only after we enter the bright sunshine of reality do I happen to glance up at the signboard above the door. It reads: Pinocchio's Café.

It is the last Friday in November, and we have been in Australia for seven weeks. Linda is sitting in the living room, reading the arts section of the *Sydney Morning Herald*, while I am at the kitchen table, deeply immersed in the crime section, which fills a large part of the paper every day. It seems there is an arsonist on the loose, setting fires in the various parks around Sydney. So far, there has been a lot of parkland destroyed, but fortunately, few buildings or people have been harmed, thanks largely to the tireless work of the volunteer bush-fire services. Police, who have few leads, are appealing to the public to be vigilant for strange behaviour. What constitutes strange arsonist behaviour, I wonder? Do they fill their Slurpee cups with gasoline at the 7-Eleven?

"There's an Andy Warhol exhibition on," says Linda.

"*Humn*?" I always say this when I'm pretending I haven't heard something I don't want to hear.

"Andy Warhol. It starts today."

"I hate Andy." Here's a guy who made himself famous with ink screens of soup cans; when it comes to the top yo-yos of art, I figure he comes second only to the Dada surrealist Marcel Duchamp, who turned a urinal upside down and called it a fountain.

"*Humn*?" Linda gets up to brush her hair and put on some lipstick. "Hurry up. I want to catch the 10:10 ferry."

The Museum of Contemporary Art is in an old customs building that squats, in art-deco fashion, adjacent to Circular Quay. As we pull into the ferry terminal, a large banner proclaims Andy's presence or, since he has been thankfully dead for several years, the presence of his artwork. We follow the shoreline around the cove, pay our fares, and enter. I must say, they've done a fine job of renovating the building into an art gallery. The morbid scent of bureaucracy still weighs heavily in the air, but the decor has been considerably lightened up and, of course, bilious green linoleum is the new black.

Andy's exhibit is on the second floor, cunningly situated at the end of the permanent collection. Since it's on the way, we decide we might as well see what's contemporary south of the equator these days. The first room we enter is painted completely white and is utterly devoid of anything except for a set of wall brackets on one wall, holding up a simple plank shelf. Upon the shelf rest some twenty snap-lid glass jars, the sort that baby food comes in. Inside each jar is a crumpled Kleenex. "It looks like snot rags in a jar," I say. "What's it called?"

Linda reads the card attached to the wall. "*Snot Rags in a Jar*."

Well, you can't say Australian artists lack a sense of humour. I don't even dare stay for a moment longer, lest I be consumed by an overwhelming urge to contribute a booger, and we flee to the adjacent room. This turns out to be a mistake. It is filled with ping-pong balls, hanging by threads from the ceiling in an undulating wave. I walk beneath, in heaven, deeley-bopping them with the tips of my fingers, until Linda grabs me by the collar and pulls me out.

We continue on into a largish room, featuring kitchen

cupboards painted in riotous fashion and numerous other "mixed media." My favourite is a muddy truck tire with a broken two-by-four shoved through a hole in the tread. By now, we are getting into the swing of things, and when we spot a fire extinguisher embedded in a red niche, we stop to admire it. "What an intriguing concept," Linda exclaims. "What do you think it's trying to say?"

I place my hand upon my chin and stare pensively for a moment. "Perhaps, it's not trying to say anything. Perhaps it's just meant to *be*."

Linda nods. "To be, or not to be. That *is* the question."

It doesn't take long for this sort of behaviour to attract attention, and a security guard appears on the horizon. He is dressed in a pair of grey slacks and a burgundy shirt that complements the linoleum and around his waist is a heavy utility belt from which a flashlight, used perhaps to illuminate bewildered patrons, dangles. He is whispering into a walkie-talkie as he heads our way. We duck down a hallway, slip into a side room, and wait silently as he passes by. As soon as he is gone, I note that we are in an exhibit of quilts. One piece is done up in black-and-white squares, like a chessboard, onto which several red, blue, and yellow pillows have been placed. Much to our delight, we discover that the pillows are attached simply by Velcro and are busily rearranging them when the guard catches us. "All right, you two!" He frog-marches us, giggling, to the exit and unceremoniously throws us out. All in all, it is the best Andy Warhol exhibition I have never attended.

Pondering contemporary art is thirsty work, and we set off to find somewhere suitable to slake our palates. We head back along Circular Quay, circling the cove toward the Sydney Opera House on the far point. We are almost to the opera house when we pass a small, brick-and-tile building, adjacent to the water. It is the former harbourmaster's office, now converted to a café. One side is festooned with large, white umbrellas, and a sandwich board invites us to come into the Oyster Bar and sample the seafood platter.

Hugh, our waiter, leads us to a white-plastic table near the water. Directly across the cove is Sydney Harbour Bridge. As we await our drinks, ferries zip in and out of the quay in a bustling way, which contrasts nicely with our own sloth. Hugh soon returns with a bottle of Chardonnay and a selection of seafood on a platter of crushed ice. The prawns are truly heroic in size, and the mussels, scallops, and smoked salmon tasty indeed. We have such a merry time that, upon Hugh's suggestion, we purchase tickets for the Oyster Bar's New Year's Eve celebration next month, which includes a seafood dinner, complimentary bubbly, and an unrestricted view of the Harbour Bridge fireworks.

We reluctantly bid adieu to Hugh and make our, somewhat wobbly, way back to the Manly Ferry wharf. It is only after the cool harbour breeze sobers me up that I realize the significance of Hugh's invitation—it is less than a month to Christmas. ■

CHAPTER 6

Christmas Down Under

G'day," says the TV meteorologist. His name is Guy, and he sports a set of teeth that would do a hippo proud. He points to a weather map covered in bright yellow sun symbols. "Weather conditions for Sydney on December the first are mainly fine." He clicks his little remote and the picture doesn't change. "Conditions will continue to be mostly fine for tomorrow (click), and the next day (click), and the next." He finishes clicking, and Biff the anchorman smiles hugely, as well. "Thanks, Guy. Now, back to the Sydney arsonist." I turn off the TV before I contract diabetes.

It is only 9:00 AM and already it's thirty degrees Celsius and too hot for a run. I stare out the patio door at the incredibly white sandy beach stretching before me. All my life, I have yearned to have Christmas in the sun, and now here I am—it is hot, it is balmy, and, frankly, it is creeping me out. I turn to Linda, who is standing in the kitchen, with a knife and a pile of strawberries, melon slices, and mangoes, preparing a bowl of fruit salad for breakfast. Her diet is doing wonders for her figure. "Is it just me, or do you feel odd about all this?"

Linda glances up briefly toward the bright, sunny beach. "It's you."

"Seriously, don't you miss the snow and roasting chestnuts by the open fire and all that Christmassy stuff?"

Linda peels and dices a mango. "Nope. I could live here forever. I love it."

I stare out at the swaying Norfolk pines. "I guess I'm just

homesick for winter."

"No, you're just crazy. Here, have some fruit salad." I pull up a chair, but no sooner do we sit down at the table than the phone rings. It is Jeanne, back in Calgary, where it's still yesterday afternoon. She is calling to let us know that all our friends back home have sent us a care package full of goodies. "The post office promised it would be there by Christmas, so keep an eye out for it," she says. "We love you and miss you."

After she hangs up, Linda makes a decision. "I know what'll cheer you up. Let's go shopping."

In Canada, of course, all the retail outlets have been kitted out with Christmas decorations since Labour Day. Up until now, however, there has been a distinct lack of commercial effort on the part of their Oz counterparts, but given that December has arrived, we expect that the appropriate attitude will emerge. After breakfast, we set off for the Corso in high spirits.

Unfortunately, our search along the pedestrian way uncovers nary a neon Santa or a Disney character dressed in elf costume, although the newsagent has a nice collection of surreal greeting cards. I especially like the one with Godzilla consuming Santa's reindeer; I suppose it's a break from eating Japanese all the time.

We return home to the Seaview, confused about where to satisfy our yuletide urges. Gertrude is in the hallway, busily hanging a holiday wreath on her door. "You want to go to Warringah Mall," she says. "They have oodles of that sort of crap." We thank her and set off in the afternoon for this Mecca of Christianity.

After travelling by bus for some distance along Pittwater Road, a large commercial establishment appears on our left. Australians generally hate to shop, and one look at Warringah Mall gives us all the reasons why. It is the sort of place one might expect from an architect on LSD—one side looks more or less conventional, but around the corner, it aimlessly meanders off in all directions and colours. We wander, lost and confused, through several levels until we stumble upon a Woolworth's department store. We inquire within, and a clerk directs us to the special Christmas section. When we finally find the display, it consists of three strings of blinking lights, two boxes of tree decorations, and one plaster bust of Jesus, gazing piously at a partridge tree. I feel like weeping.

"Don't you understand the *purpose* of Christmas?" I ask a passing clerk.

"What's wrong, love?"

"*Look* at this stuff." I point around the store. "There're no decorations or lights, there's not even carol music."

The clerk snaps her fingers. "*That's* what I forgot. Hang on a sec, sugar." She rushes off to a backroom, and the store speakers suddenly come to life with Bob Marley singing "White Christmas." When she returns, she has a big smile on her face. "Now, doesn't that make you feel more like Christmas?" Frankly, it makes me feel like stoking up a yuletide spliff.

We check out a few more stores but, except for a pair of flip-flops the shape of yule logs and some Balinese shadow puppets dancing around the North Pole in a window display, there's not a spot of holiday cheer to be seen. When I contemplate buying the Jesus bust and making a halo for him out of a string of lights, Linda steers me toward the bus stop.

By the time we return home, I'm too tired and dispirited to cook, so we opt for a roast-chicken takeaway, locally known as the chuck shop. Inside, dozens of flightless carcasses rotate in front of an electric element that could double as a steel smelter. I immediately begin to wilt when I step through the door, but Señora Fortado, from Portugal, is unfazed as she bags a bird, then throws in some roast potatoes, two cobs of corn, and a large container of gravy for me. "There you are," she cheerfully says, as she hands over the food. Despite the lovely smell, I can't generate any real enthusiasm, and Mama spots this. "What's wrong, Hon?"

"It just doesn't feel like Christmas, Señora."

"Oh, I will fix that." She reaches beneath the counter and pulls out a bright red hat, with a white fringe and a pompom on the tip. "Here is my gift to you." She comes around the counter and plants it on my head. "There, you look just like Santa now." I look in a mirror on the wall, and sure enough, there's St. Nick, in shorts and flip-flops, beaming back at me. I give her a hug and head back home to dinner. I guess some folks around here do know how to do Christmas, after all.

The shadow puppets we saw remind me that Greg and Heather should be back from Bali by now. A few days later, I give Greg a call. "How was your honeymoon?" I ask.

"Brilliant. Come and stay the night at our place. I'll cook you dinner and we'll tell you all about it."

That Saturday afternoon, we pack an overnight bag, take the ferry into Circular Quay, and then catch the suburban rail line to Marrickville. A century or so ago, Marrickville was a vibrant working-class neighbourhood, home to the families of carpenters who worked in the surfboard factories down by the docks. But after the Second World War, surfboard production shifted offshore to fibreglass plants in Taiwan and the factories were shuttered up. Those who could afford it drifted off to the endless suburbs that stretch for miles to the west; those who couldn't remained there, collecting the dole and drinking Woodpecker cider by the quart.

The train station, an aging brick structure, is decorated in a surprisingly diverse and colourful range of coarse graffiti, giving it a somewhat festive, if vulgar, air. As Linda and I walk the few blocks to Greg's, we can't help but notice the impressive number of cars sitting on blocks, *sans* wheels. Either folks around here have an affection for brake pads or there's been a run on rubber-jacking.

Greg's street is a quiet lane, lined on both sides with brick row houses dating from the turn of the twentieth century. Some, I notice, are boarded up and abandoned, but the ones clustered around

Greg's home appear to be well kept, with painted sills, clean front yards, and flower boxes overflowing with geraniums and petunias.

Greg answers the door and greets us with a big hug. "Welcome to Marrickville!" he enthuses.

"What's with all the cars with no tires?"

Greg waves a dismissive hand. "Oh, that. Just some kids' idea of fun."

I point to Heather's car, a late-model Japanese import, out front. "Aren't you afraid they'll pinch yours?"

"Nope. I've got theft-proof lugnuts. They're too dumb to figure out how to get them off."

Greg's home is cool and quiet, in sharp contrast to the outside. The floors and wainscoting are a deep mahogany colour, and the plastered walls are painted in celadon green. Antique oriental rugs, Greg's passion, are placed throughout the living and dining rooms, and the walls are decorated with festive Balinese masks. All in all, the house has a jewel-box quality to it, helped, no doubt, by the fact that it is no more than three metres wide.

Heather appears from the kitchen, carrying a pitcher of ice-cold lemonade, and we all move to the rear of the house. Heather loves animals—part of the reason for purchasing their home was so that she can have a dog—and as we exit the back door, we are greeted by Poppy, their rambunctious golden Labrador puppy, who makes our acquaintance with a tongue dipped in slobber. The backyard is a tiny space, some six metres deep and enclosed by a tall, wooden fence. We sit at a table beneath a large umbrella, from which Greg gives us a brief horticultural tour. In addition to a row of tomatoes along one side of the fence, he has planted numerous herbs and spices, including a small tree that produces Kaffir lime leaves. "I've never heard of them," I say. "What do they taste like?"

"You'll find out later," Greg promises.

Our conversation is interrupted by screeching tires and the metallic smack of a rear-ender outside, followed shortly by several people shouting loudly in various Asian dialects. Ignoring the distraction, I ask Greg, "What made you decide on Marrickville?"

"It's a brilliant area," explains Greg. "There're all kinds of ethnic grocery stores and restaurants—it's a real up-and-coming neighbourhood. Everyone wants to live here; it's only a few kilometres from the centre of town. You can literally walk to work."

I personally wouldn't want to walk anywhere in Marrickville without a chainsaw slung over my shoulder. "How much did you pay for your home?" I ask.

"Just a quarter of a million," says Greg proudly.

Lemonade squirts out my nose. "*How* much?" I could buy two homes of the same quality in most cities in Canada for that price.

"Not to worry, mate, it'll be worth four times that one day."

I decide to check Greg's medicine cabinet at the earliest possible moment. In the meantime, he goes into the kitchen and fetches out a large book. "Do you like Thai food?"

"Of course."

"No, I mean *real* Thai food." He hands me a large tome entitled *Thailand: The Beautiful Cookbook*, by Panurat Poladitmontri and Judy Lew. The authors have collected more than one hundred recipes, covering everything from vegetable curries to barbecued pork, grilled fish, and stir-fried chicken. It is beautifully illustrated, with not only the dishes, but also scenes from marketplaces, villages, and temples. "I think you'll enjoy a few of these beauties," says Greg.

"Just the look of the book is enough to make me hungry," I say. "I'm going to get my own copy someday."

Dinner that evening lives up to all expectations. The appetizer is cubed pork, boiled in a reduction of sweet soy sauce, caramelized sugar, fish sauce, and shallots. Greg serves it directly from the pot, each cube skewered onto a long, bamboo sliver. It is the most tender, truly succulent meat I've ever eaten. "What part of the pig is this?" I ask.

"The neck," replies Greg.

The next course is a salad, a mix of bean sprouts, mango, chopped red onion, romaine lettuce, and crunchy rice noodles, accompanied by a dressing made of rice vinegar, fish sauce, and sugar. Each serving is topped by crushed peanuts and finely chopped red chilies. It is sublime. "You can't possibly top this!" I exclaim.

"You wait," says Greg. The main course is red curry chicken, cubes of chicken breast and mushrooms heated in a mix of coconut milk, fish sauce, brown sugar, and red curry paste. Greg pours the mixture onto a bed of rice, then places the dish before me. An exquisite aroma arises from the plate, caressing my nostrils.

"What's that smell?" I ask.

"That's the Kaffir lime. It's just for flavour—don't eat it."

It definitely reminds me of lime, but the intensity of the aroma far surpasses the citrus fruit and it combines with the other ingredients to create a nasal symphony of classic proportions. I eagerly dig in, and it is only with the greatest self-control that I avoid licking the plate.

After dinner, we relax in the living room where, over a bottle of well-aged Australian Merlot, Greg and Heather show us the photos they took in Indonesia. I must confess, I'd rather bob for apples in a piranha tank than look at holiday snaps, but their enthusiasm for Bali, and the colourful photos of village processions and rice fields, holds my attention for the better part of an hour.

"Now that the honeymoon's over, what's the next step?" I ask Greg.

"I'd like to open a café in Marrickville."

I'm thinking a clothing shop with a nice line of bulletproof vests might be a better idea, but stick to the script. "You mean like a Starbucks?"

"No! A *real* café, with an espresso machine and coffee blended right on the premises."

By this time, it is quite late, and Greg escorts us up to the guest room. Or, to be more exact, the guest closet—I have owned carry-on luggage that was larger. There is room for little more than a single bed and a side table.

"Where am I supposed to sleep?" I ask.

"Right there," says Greg. "Don't worry, you'll both be comfy as a bug in a rug."

Well, *I* would be any way. Once Greg departs, I settle onto the Persian carpet on the floor. "Will you be able to sleep?" asks Linda.

"Don't worry, I'll be fine." And I am, until about 1:00 AM, when last call sounds at the local pub and I am awakened by about a dozen or so lads laughing and banging on something out on the street. It sounds like Fort Whoop-Up the night the whisky wagon offered discounts. I stuff the pillow over my head and silently wish the revellers a close encounter with a steamroller.

I awaken shortly after dawn, the abstract design of the Persian rug imprinted firmly in my face. Somewhere on the main floor, Poppy is whining to be let out for her morning constitutional. I pull on my trousers and join Greg downstairs, where he is brewing a pot of coffee. "How did you sleep?" he asks.

"Have you ever heard the expression 'I slept like the dead'?"

"Sure."

"Well, I slept like the *un*dead. Some morons were partying out on the street till three."

"That's funny, I didn't hear a thing."

"You know, you really should think about getting out of this neighbourhood sooner than later."

"Don't be such a worrywart." Greg opens the front door to let Poppy out and stops dead in his tracks. I come out onto the porch to see what the matter is—Heather's car is up on blocks, the tires completely gone.

Greg stares at the de-treaded vehicle for a long moment, then finally turns to me. "On the other hand, maybe Manly could use a good cup of coffee."

Compared to Greg and Heather's neighbourhood, their friends Alex and Jenny live in paradise. Both are schoolteachers, and since classes are out for summer vacation, they invite us to their home for lunch. They love the outdoors, and their house, about eight kilometres due west of our home in Manly, backs onto the Garigal, an urban incursion of the national park north of Sydney. The sweet smell of the forest hangs in the air and the hustle and bustle of the city is a distant murmur. It is an idyllic scene, except for what sounds like a group of madmen laughing hysterically in the trees.

"Watch this," says Alex. He holds out a half-dozen sunflower seeds in the palm of his hand, and a laughing kookaburra swoops down and lands on his thumb. The bird is a chubby ball of fur, with a large beak and a thick skull. I am told they like to nest in tree hollows, but if none is available, they will create their own by crashing headfirst into a termite nest, knocking themselves silly in the process. The kookaburra daintily picks a few seeds out of Alex's hand, then flies off. Almost immediately, a hurtling ball of colourful feathers careens onto the patio and tries to land on his hand. It is a rainbow lorikeet, with green wings, blazing red breast, blue head, and red beak. Before it can snatch any seeds, however, Alex jerks his hand away, and the bird reels off in frustration.

"You're not allowed to feed lorikeets," he explains. "They get unhealthy and their babies are born with tiny wings." As they scramble across the forest floor, the deformed lorikeets, called "runners," are easy prey for feral cats.

In addition to birds, Australia's national forest reserves host a wide variety of wildlife, most of which seems to come to some form of gruesome demise. The echidna, a porcupine-like ball of spiny fur, is often spotted as road pizza on the highways that criss-cross its native habitat. The bandicoot, a nocturnal mammal with a long nose for rooting out termites, tends to become owl chow. My favourite is the sugar glider, a flying squirrel that can glide some fifty metres from one tree to the next, using skin sails stretched between its front and back legs. Aborigines consider them a light snack.

Perhaps the most distinctive feature of this national forest reserve is the abundant eucalyptus. I am a great admirer of this native Australian tree—not only does its bark peel off in great leprous lengths, but it is also one of the most obnoxious plants ever conceived. Having first evolved some fifty million years ago, when the continents formed one great land mass, it was banished by continental drift to Australia, where it immediately took up residence in all the best ecosystems. It is, of course, redolent with oil, which is fine in cough-drop dosages but is extremely lethal in concentrated form. If that's not enough, it is the arboreal equivalent of the Molotov cocktail, its peeling bark perfectly designed to accelerate brush fires from their relatively benign low level of conflagration up into the top-most crowns, where it proves unerringly fatal to other tree species. During times of drought, it tends to shed branches to conserve moisture, a rather unfortunate habit if you happen to be passing below. Australians talk of the drop bear, a carnivorous koala that hides in the branches of the eucalyptus and hunts by leaping down upon unsuspecting prey and knocking it senseless.

In short, the eucalyptus is the grinch of the forest and, of course, living adjacent to this grinch has its problems. It hasn't rained in the last fortnight, and the countryside has taken on the general demeanor of Melba toast. I note the proximity of a half-dozen or so eucalyptus trees to Alex and Jenny's property. "Do you think your house is safe?" I ask.

"It is as long as the arsonists don't come along."

"I've been reading about them in the papers." Several days before, a fire had swept through a western suburb, and two people had narrowly escaped death by taking refuge in their swimming pool. "I hope the police catch them."

Alex turns to his two young children, who are cheerfully playing with their toys on the patio. "Yeah, so do we."

Later that afternoon, after we've returned to our apartment in Manly, the arsonists are still on our minds. Linda focuses her attention on the vivid rendition of a bush fire on our living-room wall. "It looks as though it was painted by someone in a lunatic asylum."

The painting appears to be firmly bolted onto the wall, but when I fiddle around with the frame, I discover it is mounted on a sliding hook and comes off relatively easily. Unfortunately, it is covering up a sizeable hole in the wall where, judging by the encircling brown splash marks, some previous tenant apparently attempted to kill a cockroach by hurling a bottle of beer at it. "Maybe I should just put it back," I offer.

Linda shakes her head. "We'll find something to replace it."

We head to the harbour end of the Corso to a large framing shop. The outlet is crammed with a wide assortment of posters, and we eagerly dig through the stacks. Linda finds a charming study of delectable fruit sitting in a bowl, painted by Henri Matisse. I come across a reproduction of Van Gogh's epic painting *Terrace Café at Night*, featuring the warm glow of an outdoor café in the cobbled main square of Arles in southern France. The surrounding streets, shadowed in shades of blue and violet, remind me of the jacaranda petals carpeting the streets in Manly. Van Gogh's sky is filled with bright silvery swirls of stars—the first time he used that technique in a painting. It was finished in 1888, right about the time he lopped his ear off and sent it as a gift to a rather surprised prostitute. "I like this one," I announce.

"It's beautiful," responds Linda. "We'll get both."

We hang the Matisse poster above the dining-room table, there to whet our appetites. The Van Gogh is mounted on the bracket vacated by our forest fire. I must say that the result is much cheerier. I guess it's all in knowing how to pick the right lunatic.

Brightly lit forests remind me it is time to buy a Christmas tree.

After our experience at Warringah Mall, it comes as no surprise that no one sells them hereabouts. The Norfolk pines in front of the Seaview fit the general ticket, but it's difficult to squeeze a thirty-metre-tall tree into an apartment, even sideways. I decide instead to decorate a corn plant left by the previous tenant. The shrub in question stands about a metre tall and appears to have been chewed upon by corn bats, but other than that, it is in good repair. I cut several large snowflakes out of gold foil and use bits of sticky tack to attach them to the plant. I am just putting the finishing touches on the tree, when Linda returns from the foyer. "Any mail today?" I ask.

She tosses a pile of letters onto the coffee table. "Just some bills."

I'm beginning to get a bit worried. It's less than a week to the twenty-fifth, and there's been nary a sign of our care package from Canada. "I guess we'll have to make inquiries."

It is blazing hot outside as we make our way toward the Manly Post Office. We dodge from side to side of the street, trying to make the most of any patches of shade we find beneath the scented magnolia trees, but by the time we reach our destination, we are drenched in sweat. The interior of the building is an oasis of cool air conditioning, however, and for once we are happy to stand in line waiting to be served. The clerk who serves us is dressed in a sharply pressed shirt and shorts and sports a tiny wisp of hair on the top of his skull, which he pats occasionally to reassure himself it hasn't blown off.

Linda explains that our expected Christmas parcel has failed to turn up.

"Are there any flammable objects, explosives, toxic chemicals, or corrosive substances in your parcel?" he asks.

Linda rolls her eyes. "If there were, it wouldn't exactly make it a pleasant Christmas surprise, would it?"

The clerk purses his lips, then disappears for several minutes. He returns with a stack of paper the size of the *Sydney Yellow Pages* and slides them across the counter. "We'll need you to fill out a few forms so that we can initiate a trace."

Linda stares at the paper. "How long will it take?"

The clerk glances at his watch. "About six weeks."

I gather in the pile of forms. "Good. We should have the paper-work done by then." We head for a side desk to begin the task.

Christmas Eve arrives, and it is sweltering. It is the last day for shopping at the grocery stores—the part of Christmas that *isn't* ignored around here is the day off—and I still haven't decided what to cook for Christmas Day. Popping a turkey in the oven for three hours is the last thing on my mind. "What would you like, instead?" I ask Linda.

"Why don't we do what everyone else in Oz does? Let's have shrimp."

I think this an excellent idea and immediately head out to get the main ingredient. Our fishmonger is located at the ferry marina in Manly Harbour, his outlet little more than a large, stainless-steel counter filled with ice and the day's catch. The fish is very fresh and his prices are quite reasonable, so for the last few weeks, I've been buying an assortment of tuna, white fish, and whatever else he has that is just off the boat. I peer at the chalkboard to see what's available today and literally rub my eyes in disbelief—the price of shrimp has doubled from the week before. "What's going *on*?" I ask.

The monger, who is desultorily chopping the heads off salmon with a large cleaver, shrugs his shoulders. "There's been a typhoon in Thailand. Hell of a mess, mate, nothing we can do about it."

I grumble as I pay and, despite the flawless blue sky, a black cloud is still hovering over my head when I arrive back at the Seaview.

"Well, Merry Christmas to you," says Gertrude, as I sullenly exit the elevator.

"Sorry, I'm just mad because I think I'm getting ripped off." I explain the mysterious price rise of shrimp.

Gertrude smiles. "Well, you shouldn't feel so suspicious that you're getting ripped off."

"No?"

"No. You *are* getting ripped off. Those *bleddy* pirates double up the price of shrimp *every* year. It's a tradition, you know."

I feel strangely relieved. No sooner have I put the shrimp in the fridge than Linda rushes in, waving a postal-delivery notice. "It's here!"

The post office closes at noon, so we scurry down as quickly as possible. We get inside with several minutes to spare, much to the chagrin of the employee standing at the door. As luck would have it, our prim little clerk is behind the counter, this time, beaming as we approach. He takes our card and disappears into the back, returning a few minutes later with a package that has been placed in a large, plastic bag. Even through the bag, it is plain that its brown-paper covering has been torn open.

"It appears to have been damaged slightly," he concedes.

I stare at the package. "It looks like a crocodile flossed his teeth with it."

The clerk purses his lips again. "Well, if you have an *issue*, there are forms you can fill out."

I take the parcel in my hands. "Forget it. I'd rather kiss the croc than spend Christmas with you."

With the package cradled in my arms, we hurry back home and carefully open the box. To our relief, nothing seems to be damaged. Inside is a lovely pair of mittens, a wool scarf, two pairs of long johns, and a coupon for free snow-tire installation. We are delighted to see that our friends retain their sense of humour.

Best of all is a box of chocolates from a Belgian chocolatier. We eagerly crack open the gold-lamé wrapping and we each pop a bonbon filled with buttery cream into our mouth—and immediately spit it out, our tongues covered in putrid slime. Just a suggestion: never send a box of chocolates across the sweltering equator by boat.

We celebrate Christmas Day on the beach, wearing nothing but our bathing suits and our Santa hats. The beach is crowded with revellers in similar attire. Many have packed a picnic lunch of potato salad, cold cuts, and fruit salad, all washed down with bubbly.

After a few hours of sun, we return to our home, where I marinate the shrimp in crushed garlic, olive oil, and rosemary. I don't have a barbecue, but the gas stove is equipped with a clever broiler that shoots a jet of flame down onto the skewered shrimp. I serve the shrimp on a bed of rice herbed with fresh basil, green onions, and tarragon, and we retire to the balcony with a fine bottle of Chardonnay.

As the sun dips to the west and a tiny sliver of moon rises to the east, we toast the birth of Jesus and the invention of vineyards.

Some experts attribute the origin of New Year's Eve festivities to the celebration that is held the evening prior to the circumcision of Christ, as is traditional Jewish custom. Others say it started with an ancient Druid ritual during which warriors painted each other blue, drank intoxicating beverages made from fermented sheep's milk, and then charged naked through the woods to ward off evil spirits.

If you've ever been to Australia, of course, you tend to opt for the latter. Our evening starts off staidly enough, with a ride across Sydney Harbour in the *JetCat*, the ferry skimming across the placid waters toward Circular Quay. The night, which arrives relatively early even near the summer solstice, is clear and warm and filled with a multitude of stars.

Linda and I are dressed in our nattiest evening T-shirts, featuring, in my case, a stylized mosquito cartoon character named Mozz, and in Linda's, an abstract crocodile emblazoned across her bosom. Our fellow revellers tend to favour a wide assortment of festive wear, which, if they had any trait in common, would be a relative resistance to beer stains. As far as I can tell, the customary nautical drink appears to be Foster's, applied liberally onto the region nearest the mouth orifice. This is followed by the rendition of a chorus or two from popular rugby songs, involving fornication with barnyard animals. The dolphins that habitually follow the *JetCat* enter into the festive mood, merrily dodging empty cans as they are jettisoned into the wake.

As we near Circular Quay, Sydney Opera House comes into view on our left, its arching roof bathed with light and shadow to cleverly evoke the scene in *La Bohème* in which a family of giant clams rises from the primordial ooze and sings an aria. We pull into the wharf and make our way toward the opera house, along with a huge crush of people intent upon enjoying a free evening of music and fireworks. Our destination, however, is the Oyster Bar, located just to the south. The patio area has been enclosed by a steel hurricane fence, and a security guard who could pass for a large home appliance checks our tickets at the entrance before allowing us in.

We are escorted to a large table, where we are introduced to our three companions for the evening: Sheila, Judy, and Marsha. They are in their early thirties and, surprisingly, relatively sober. I can tell immediately that they are very refined, indeed, as they are drinking their beer from glasses, something that only Queen Elizabeth does with any frequency in Oz. We order Chardonnay and chat amiably, until a platter the size of a tractor hubcap arrives, covered with raw oysters and immense shrimp tails. The owners of the establishment have obviously decided that the average patron is grossly underweight, and it is only through heroic measures that we are able to ensure that no crustacean has died in vain.

A few minutes before midnight, the waiters clear away dinner and then pour everyone a glass of bubbly. Since French authorities forbid anyone to use the term "Champagne" for any wine not fermented in that specific region of France, the locals refer to it as *shampagne*. Along with the thousands of people who line the quay, we count down the few remaining seconds of the year. Precisely at midnight, a cascade of fireworks turns Harbour Bridge into a sparkling white rendition of Niagara Falls. This is followed by a vast halo of red, which glows across the entire top of the arch, as well as accompanying bursts of blue, gold, and white above the opera house. A tide of "*Ooh*," followed by "*Aah*," flows around the harbour, as everyone gapes in wonder. The spectacle goes on for a good half-hour, each display outdoing the last. A flurry of fireballs and thunderous claps mark the finale. Linda and I clink glasses and kiss, then wish ourselves an even better year ahead.

Sheila, Judy, and Marsha decide to stay on at the Oyster Bar and have a few more rounds. We wish them a Happy New Year, then, amid the drifting gunpowder smoke, we make our way back to the wharf. The wind has picked up, and the ferry ride back to Manly is marked by choppy seas. The revellers on board, by this time fortified with prodigious amounts of lager, forego their rugby songs in favour of decorating the hull of the *JetCat* with curry and digestive fluids. When we arrive at the Manly dock, we slip and slide our way down the wharf to terra firma and make our way toward the Corso.

The pedestrian mall is crammed with thoroughly snozzled folk, many of them singing the vowels to "Auld Lang Syne." We bob our way through, carefully stepping over several celebrants who have decided that a cobble pathway is an excellent locale for a face-down nap. Near the Steyne Hotel, two groups of Manly youth have gathered to express their mutual dislike by hurling cans of ale at each other. The police consider this a terrible waste of beer and charge in to rearrange some coiffures with their truncheons. A melee soon ensues, much to the delight of spectators, and several articles of street furniture are festively dislodged and hurled into the sea. We bid the rioters adieu as they are carted off in a Black Maria and return to the Seaview.

Linda heads for bed, but I discover a nicely chilled bottle of previously unmolested wine in the fridge. I pull the cork, tuck it under my arm, and find a comfortable chair on the balcony. Between sips, I stare out at the stars and listen to the waves crashing below. Chardonnay always puts me in a philosophical mood, and I soon find myself musing upon the vagaries of life.

It is only nine months since we decided to quit our jobs, sell our house, and run away, yet it seems like we are light-years away from the chilly confines of Canada. A luminous warmth envelopes me as I contemplate tropical beaches, the excitement of Sydney, and the weird things living in palm trees. So much more happens here than back home, but could we see ourselves living in Manly for the rest of our lives? My thoughts are interrupted when I discover that the contents of the bottle have mysteriously evaporated. I place it gently on the balcony floor tiles, shushing it when it noisily rolls over on its side. I make a solemn resolution: the New Year will be a time to sober up and make important, life-altering decisions, preferably in that order. ∎

CHAPTER 7

Little Penguins
and Skinks

Just south of Manly is North Head, a massive block of rock marking the northern side of the entrance to Sydney Harbour. Considering that it is in the midst of Australia's largest city, it is a wild and spectacular place, covered in sand dunes, forest, and scrub, and isolated from the greater community for centuries due to a curious combination of geography and circumstances.

From the first European occupation of the area, military commanders were intrigued by the defensive capabilities of North Head. In 1790, Governor Arthur Phillip reconnoitred the region, but he was speared by Aborigines when he stopped at a whale barbecue on the beach. Plans for military installations were subsequently shelved in favour of a quarantine station, which was completed just in time to be inaugurated by a smallpox pandemic. For more than a century, aside from syphilitic seamen and the occasional leper, North Head remained relatively uninhabited, until just before the Second World War, when the Australian government built an artillery station on the site.

After the war, the area was opened up for recreational purposes, under the apparent assumption that people would be delighted to flock to a quarantine zone studded with unexploded ammunition. Today, hikers can follow pathways around the two-square-kilometre site, taking in the amazing views of the harbour and the city, the solitude, the immensity of the ocean and the sky, and, aside from the sewage-treatment plant located nearby, the unsullied natural habitat.

Mind you, it's too bloody hot to do that today, so I opt instead for a morning walk to nearby Shelley Beach. Located just south of Manly Beach proper, Shelley is tucked into a charming, shady cove. I am told there is excellent scuba diving in the bay, but I have come here today in search of little penguins.

The scientific name for these creatures is *Eudyptula minor*, but Manly residents call them "little penguins" because they are, well, little. Other than that, they apparently conform to the usual penguiny norm, having white tummies, stubby, flightless wings, black posteriors, and waddly gaits. My purpose in seeking out the little penguins is twofold: first, to satisfy my inner geek, which has never seen a penguin in the wild and, second, to make some effort to become acquainted with the indigenous marine wildlife, and since this boils down to either great white sharks, bluebottles, or little penguins, I have opted for the latter.

When I reach Shelley Beach, a group of surfers is just heading round the far point for Fairy Bower, a portion of North Head exposed to the strong surf of the Pacific Ocean. Several families have set up umbrellas, their small children playing beneath them with the shells that litter the strand.

I approach a woman wearing a print muumuu and ask her where I might spot a little penguin. Rather than pointing out to sea, she directs me to a cliff of damp sandstone, the base of which has been eroded to a thin, deep crevasse. When I bend over and peer into the opening, I can hear encouraging peeps and pick up the smell of what I guess to be penguin poo, but the recesses of the crevasse are simply too dark to spot anything. I attempt to woo them forth by waving a piece of anchovy-flavoured pizza crust, fished from a nearby litter bin, and making kissy noises, but despite my best efforts, they fail to respond. I finally give up when passersby start to point and whisper, and head back home, distinctly disappointed with my little penguin-spotting expedition. As I walk along the esplanade, I find my funk surprising. After all, what have I got to be blue about? Living in Manly is a breeze, the weather's lovely, the people are delightful, and we don't have a care in the world. So what if I didn't see little penguins today—I can come back any time I wish.

Or can I? Maybe that's what's bothering me. Ever since the turn of the new year, the inevitable passage of time has been niggling at the back of my mind. I've been trying to suppress it, but the day may come when we have to move on. Even though it's a hot day, a chill passes over me, as if a cloud has wandered in front of the sun.

When I arrive at the Seaview, Gertrude is in the foyer, checking her morning mail. Today's delivery includes several bills and a menu flyer for a vegetarian restaurant promoting 10 per cent off curried mung beans, a surefire way of shifting those appetizing puppies out the door if I ever heard one. I suspect the restaurant owner might have more success offering a 110 per cent discount. I start to explain this to Gertrude, but she distracts me with a brochure for the Sydney Festival. According to the introduction, the festival is held every January and features a wide assortment of theatrical plays, films, dance, and free music performances.

I look through the itinerary. "There's jazz playing at the Domain today," I say.

"Well, then, you should pack a picnic and take your sweetheart." Gertrude winks in roguish fashion. "My Dennis used to take me dancing in the Domain. Remember to take some bubbly—you might get lucky."

That's sufficient motivation for me, and my sense of malaise immediately dissipates. Linda and I gather some cold chicken, salad, and fruit in one backpack and a blanket, cutlery, and liquid refreshments in a second. Within the hour, we arrive at Circular

Quay in central Sydney. To mark the festival, the Aboriginal man who plays his didgeridoo adjacent to the quay has forsworn his usual selection of traditional clan tunes in favour of "Basin Street Blues." We pause to donate a dollar to the cause, then continue on to our destination.

The Domain, an ancient British term for village heath or commons, is part of Royal Botanical Park, a large, open area due east of Circular Quay that is roughly the same size as Manhattan's Central Park. Sydney Opera House is at its very northern tip, with Government House, a largish pile of Gothic Revival masonry, due south on Macquarie Street.

Macquarie Street is named after Lachlan Macquarie, a British Army captain who was, by all accounts, an interesting bloke. He was appointed governor of New South Wales in 1809, after navy mutineers deposed Governor William Bligh (who seems to have suffered more than his fair share of naval mutinies, doesn't he?). As governor, he presided over the metamorphosis of a quarrelsome penal colony into a modern state and, thus, is generally considered to be the father of modern Australia. Although his name appears on just about everything short of portable toilets, probably the most interesting application of his moniker occurs due east of Government House at Mrs. Macquaries Chair. This sitting area was carved out of a rock ledge at the tip of the point overlooking the bay, so that Macquarie's wife, Elizabeth, could sit and contemplate the view.

Today, of course, you can see Harbour Bridge and the Opera House from there, but two hundred years ago neither existed, so Lady Macquarie would have had to amuse herself by gazing upon Pinchgut Island and the naval dockyards of Woolloomooloo Bay, which gives you an idea of how exciting Sydney was in those days. It is said that a wish made in her chair may be granted, but she couldn't have been wishing that her hubby would get recalled to England, since he was stuck with his job for twelve years.

We make our way in leisurely fashion southward from the chair, passing a line of Moreton Bay fig trees, which would be rather homely, with their leathery leaves and ropey trunks, were it not that they grow to a magnificent height, some to sixty metres, and create immense patches of cooling shade. Sydney-siders love them and gladly put up with their tendency to drop branches on windy days, as long as they land on someone else.

We soon discern a telltale sound—not jazz, but corks popping. We follow the din until we arrive at the Band Lawn, where thousands of people, with oodles of bubbly, are resting on the grass. We spread our blanket, unpack our own bottle of fizzy, and engage in picnicking, Oz fashion. I don't recall who performed that day, or whether they were any good, but Gertrude's advice about the bubbly was spot on. And it sure beats penguin spotting.

"Would you look at those beauties? Hang on while I pull over."

It is a Saturday morning, early in January. Greg has picked me up in his Holden step van and we are cruising near Mona Vale Beach, about ten kilometres north of Manly. The beauties that Greg has spotted are not, as you might suspect, beach babes, but rather a thick, gnarly patch of bamboo, growing out of a ditch adjacent to the highway. Greg has decided to adopt a Polynesian theme for his backyard garden, and he needs some poles as growing stakes for his tomatoes.

We clamber down from the van and Greg rummages through a tool kit in the back until he finds his machete. The tool in question is so pitted and rusty that had he told me he had pried it from the skeletal fingers of a Japanese soldier found deep in the forest highlands of Bali, I wouldn't have batted an eyelash. Holding the weapon high, he advances upon the coppice with the assurance of a man who has never used a machete in his life.

"Would you rather I did that?" I ask.

"No worries. You just keep an eye out for ditch adders."

As far as I'm concerned, the most dangerous wildlife around here is holding a machete. I stand about twelve metres away, directly behind Greg. He grips a large bamboo trunk firmly in his left hand and takes a mighty overhand swing, harmlessly grazing the tough bark of the five-metre-thick tree. I can only assume that the shock of not cutting off his thumb is so great that he loses his grip on the machete, and it arcs between my legs and skitters about fifteen metres down the road.

Greg coughs. "Perhaps I should watch for the adders."

"Good idea." I breathe slowly, hoping to relax enough for my testicles to re-descend, as I fetch the machete.

From my experience as a prospector blazing a trail through the boreal forests of northern Canada, I know that the safest axe is the sharpest axe. I root through the toolbox until I find a file and, after about five minutes of honing, return the cutting edge to its original shiny steel. I pick some thick, green offshoots, and within half an hour, we have a dozen stakes.

As we are tossing the poles into the back of the van, Greg pauses to sniff the air.

"What's wrong?" I ask.

"Can't you smell the smoke?"

I shrug. "Someone's burning rubbish."

"No." Greg casts his gaze about the horizon for a moment, but no pall of smoke is visible, so he shrugs and we get back into the van and continue our journey. As we proceed north along Highway 10, it branches off onto Barrenjoey Road and we enter a peninsula, some twelve kilometres long, where the surroundings take a definite turn for the affluent. We pass Newport Beach and Whale Beach, until we finally come to Palm Beach. Virtually every beach in Australia is public property—the natives won't have it any other way. Vistas overlooking beaches are another matter, however, especially if they are majestic, pristine, and isolated.

Palm Beach definitely qualifies on all three counts.

We park at a paved lot, don our swimsuits, and head for the water. A wide band of sugary sand stretches for several kilometres in a gentle arc, with nary a building or a structure to be seen. We dive into the surf and swim out some ninety metres. While paddling about, getting ready to catch a good wave, I glance back at the cliff behind the beach. High above, hidden among the palm trees, I see the rooftops and wide patios of stately homes. "Who lives up there?" I ask.

"Oh, iron and media barons, that sort of thing. They steal from the poor and give to the rich."

A truly excellent wave approaches and we bodysurf our way into shore. I have taken the precaution of securing my trunks with the drawstring and manage to hang onto my bathing suit. We enjoy perhaps another hour of similar sport, until the wind shifts and a pall of soot begins to settle upon the water in large, black splotches. Greg picks some off his skin and examines it closely.

"What's it from?" I ask.

"Eucalyptus bark." Greg has grown up with forest fires— most of New South Wales is plagued by hundreds of fires every year, and a huge volunteer force has evolved to battle what are mostly bush blazes. Many of the river valleys that crisscross Sydney proper have been left in their primeval state, however, and they are just as susceptible to fire as their rural counterparts. Most Sydney-siders are extremely careful when travelling in the forest regions, and firefighters are especially vigilant when thunderstorms pass through. There is only one fire source over which no one has any control—arsonists. Most years, they are nothing more than a nuisance, but this year, a combination of hot, dry weather and unrelenting winds blowing from the Outback has raised the vulnerability of Sydney.

I must admit, at this point, I am not too concerned. Having experienced forest fires in the Canadian bush, I have a rather blasé attitude—if it isn't scorching your hide, it isn't serious. Nonetheless, at Greg's insistence, we clamber out of the water, change back into our clothes, and return south. We drive for a few kilometres, but there is no imminent sign of the fire, and I convince Greg to stop at the Newport Yacht Club, a rather swank marina at which several multi-million-dollar gin palaces are moored. We order two pints of beer and sit on the patio, overlooking the marina. It is a wonderful afternoon—the sun is shining, there is a pleasant onshore breeze blowing, and I am sitting with my friend drinking an ice-cold beer. How more perfect can it get?

"Greg, tell me, are Australians generally a happy lot?"

"Nope."

"Why not? They live in a wonderful country, where everyone is far more interested in play than work."

"Doesn't stop them whining about everything."

"Like what?"

"The price of beer. Everyone complains about that."

"But everyone seems so well off. Surely there are bigger things to worry about than the price of beer."

"Sure there is." He points to the yachts moored nearby. "See them boats? Who do you think owns them?"

"Some local billionaires?"

"No, their widows."

"Oh? What happened to them?"

"They choked on their own bile when the government brought in a luxury tax."

"All of them?"

"No." Greg waves a hand vaguely in the air. "Some of these crooks croaked from apoplexy and stroke, that sort of thing." I am beginning to think that my friend holds a certain animosity for the rich, when our musings are interrupted by the wail of sirens. From where we sit, we can see the highway and we watch several emergency vehicles, including fire trucks and ambulances, go rushing by, heading south. Greg calls the waiter over. "What's happening, mate?"

"Arsonists lit fires in Ku-ring-gai and Garigal."

"Don't Alex and Jenny live near Garigal?" I ask.

"Yeah." Greg downs his pint. "Let's go."

We hop back into the van and head south on Barrenjoey until we come to the junction of Pittwater Road. Police have blocked traffic moving west toward Garigal, however. "Don't worry, I know a way round," says Greg. As a courier, he is familiar with every side road in the city, and we are soon working our way in a circuitous route toward the national park. We make steady progress until we round a corner, overlooking a deep canyon, and come to a lane lined with affluent homes, with views of the parkland. Several home owners are in their driveway, hastily loading goods into their cars, and it is easy to see why. Across the canyon, a thick pall of black smoke is billowing skyward.

An older woman is standing in her driveway, wiping tears from her eyes. We stop and help her load a few belongings into her car, until a neighbourhood warden in a red hard hat stops and orders us to clear out. We follow him back along the lane to the main road. We are among the last to leave and stop to watch the approaching smoke. Suddenly, a wall of flame thirty metres high appears at the lip of the canyon, and even at this distance, we can feel the heat on the wind that blows in our faces. We can only hope that the canyon acts as sufficient barrier to prevent it from leaping the gap. The neighbourhood warden urges us to leave.

It is obvious that the way to Garigal is barred, so we get back into the van and retreat to Pittwater Road. By the time we reach the main highway, it is packed with evacuating vehicles. A flatbed tow truck rolls past, with ten elderly men and women strapped into wheelchairs, bungeed on the back. The fire has cut off electricity, and the traffic lights have shut down. We work our way slowly south along Pittwater Road, until we reach Manly once again.

By the time we get home, the power is back on and we are able to reach Alex and Jenny by phone. Thankfully, their stretch of the Garigal was spared, and the fire front is moving away from their home. Linda and I might not be so lucky. Several hundred homes have already been destroyed, and a fire has taken hold in a portion of the forest just west of Manly. Strong winds are blowing smoke and cinders eastward toward the town, and as dark descends, the sky to the west is lit by an orange glare.

Linda stares worriedly out the patio door at the ocean, our ultimate retreat. "I can't swim," she reminds me. I hold her hand as we wait by the radio for orders to evacuate.

The orders never come. Around midnight, a weather front moves in from Tasmania, and the hot, dry wind from the west is replaced by a cold blast from the south that is accompanied by rain—at first, a light sprinkle, but soon a downpour. We awake the next morning to the aroma of soggy, burnt forest. I have never smelled anything so glorious in my life.

There's nothing like dodging imminent doom to whet the appetite. A few days later, Linda and I are invited by Bob and Margaret, friends of Greg and Heather, to that quintessential Oz cultural event, the backyard barbie. Bob is a sports nut from Vancouver, bent upon converting every Australian to that quintessential Canadian pastime—hockey. In fact, he met his wife while futilely promoting an in-line roller-skating shinny league in Melbourne some years back.

Bob and Margaret live about ten kilometres southwest of Manly, in Putney. Their home is a low, 1950s bungalow, which is in what has to be one of the ugliest suburbs I have ever seen. A bland, lifeless quadrant, the streets are lined with dusty, limp vegetation, and the blocks are dotted with identical stucco, crackerjack boxes.

Unfortunately, Putney resembles a score of other neighbourhoods in Greater Sydney; it's as if the powers-that-be decided to augment the magnificent beauty of Sydney Harbour with a garland of dead cockroaches.

Everyone lives outdoors in Oz, so it comes as no surprise to discover that Bob and Margaret's dining table is surrounded by plastic lawn chairs. The walls of the living room are decorated with a brand of plaid wallpaper designed to randomly peel off and give that Museum of Contemporary Art effect. There are no muddy tires with a two-by-four sticking out, but the hallway has a picture that bears a striking resemblance to our burning forest shack.

We pass through the kitchen into the backyard. Bob's preferred method of weed control seems to be dehydration, the lawn having the general demeanor of Death Valley. I grab a can of beer from a cooler the size of an SUV and casually glance around for rattlers. Seeing none, I advance to the end of the house, where Bob, Alex, and Greg are industriously hunched over a charcoal barbecue. It is a steel semi-globe, painted in brown enamel and mounted on a tripod—I haven't seen one like it since my dad carted ours off to the dump in his 1957 Plymouth. Bob, who is small, wiry, and exudes the general, intense air of the perpetually over-caffeinated, is busy stuffing its inner recesses with a variety of tinder, including newspaper, twigs, and a vegetarian restaurant flyer advertising curried mung beans.

"Why don't you get a gas barbecue?" I ask.

Bob glances up from his labours. "Are you kidding me? Nobody uses gas barbecues except poofters and poms." Poofters, in Aussie parlance, are homosexuals, and poms are English. It is my understanding that, around here, the terms can be used inter-changeably.

Bob's friend Shane, a charming airline purser, poofter, pom, and recently converted vegetarian rolled into one, joins us. He holds up a glass of vodka, Kahlua, and milk. "Anyone want a dirty brown cow?" Greg and Alex opt for a round, but Bob, totally absorbed, does not respond. He has finished piling in the tinder and is patiently igniting the pile on all four corners. His efforts are rewarded with a thin puff of smoke, then nothing.

"Hang on a bit, mate." Shane goes into the kitchen and returns with a bottle of duty-free, 180-proof vodka. He pours a healthy dose on the barbecue, which erupts with an impressive fireball, and we all leap back out of eyebrow-singeing range. Fortunately, there are no eucalyptus trees within ignition distance or Shane might have had to do emergency duty on a water bomber.

The barbecue eventually settles down and builds up a nice bed of glowing coals. Bob emerges with a tray of shrimp—great thick, meaty things, the size of a small lobster. Alex places them on the grill, gently turning them at intervals to ensure they are evenly cooked to a bright red sheen.

In the kitchen, Margaret has laid out all the other essentials: a big bag of corn chips, several varieties of pickle, and a large salad bowl, containing a mix of chopped cauliflower, celery, cherry tomatoes, zucchini, and several other vegetables that I can't quite identify without a DNA kit. "Interesting concoction," I say to Bob, as he enters with the shrimp. "What do you call it?

Bob picks up one of the unidentifiable items on my plate and peers at it closely. "Fridge Bottom Salad."

Everyone fills up their plates and chows down, before I take the opportunity to prepare the second course. I have brought baby lamb chops, mixed in Gord's secret lamb barbecue sauce— essentially brown sugar, soy sauce, mustard, pepper, and a hint of rosemary that I pinched off a bush in front of the Seaview. I trim off the crusty rind to expose the tender layer of fat beneath, which drips down onto the coals and flares in flashes, sending up a tantalizing aroma. I cook them just past rare to a rosy state.

Everyone is more than happy to partake of Australia's most

abundant herbivore. At this point, even Shane is dirty-brown-cowed enough that he drops the vegetarian business in favour of several helpings of lamb chops. The meal is finished off with two choices of dessert: pavlova, a traditional Oz concoction in which vanilla-flavoured egg whites and sugar are beaten to a froth, baked, and then covered with whipped cream and strawberries, and raspberry Jell-O, with baby marshmallows. Being indecisive by nature, I have both.

After the meal, Margaret, Linda, and several other guests play lawn bowling, until one of the balls gets hurled into an eavestrough by an overly enthusiastic participant trying to knock a mocking kookaburra off the roof. Bob opts for a more testosterone-based pastime. Going to the trunk of his car, he fetches a goodly number of in-line roller skates and hockey sticks, and we dragoon several neighbours, with the promise of copious amounts of lager, into a game of shinny under the streetlights. Bob is an excellent teacher, and even the rookies are soon doing quite well. Indeed, Shane proves so adept that, if it weren't for a sudden bout of diarrhea brought on by my lamb chops, his team would have beaten us soundly. As it is, we have a lovely cross-cultural mix of Foster's *Hockey Night in Oz*.

I pick up a copy of the *Sydney Morning Herald* a few days after Bob and Margaret's barbecue, and I am relieved to see that two people have been arrested in connection with the recent fire. The suspects, two young men in their late teens, apparently have a history of arson and were seen in the vicinity of the origin of the blaze. Although several dozen homes and hundreds of hectares of forest were destroyed, no one was seriously injured, and the entire city breathes a sigh of relief.

Linda and I deem it as good a time as any to check out the eucalyptus-clad Blue Mountains, just west of Sydney. Greg is more than happy to play tour guide, and on the following

Saturday, we set out in his Holden van along the Great Western Motorway. It is early in the morning, and it is cool, damp, and foggy. "Great weather for viewing mountains," says Linda.

Greg sticks his head out the window to conduct a meteorological investigation. "No worries, it'll clear."

My guidebook explains that the Blue Mountains are not, in truth, mountains at all. The area, covering more than two million square hectares, is a high sandstone plateau that's been deeply cut by rivers to create stupendous, steep-walled gorges. The plateau rises to some thirteen hundred metres, and snow is not uncommon several times a year in the higher elevations. Within its boundaries are some of the most diverse ecosystems on the planet, including the habitat for the long-nosed potaroo, a kangaroo that looks like a rat and munches on fungus. And, just a few years ago, scientists discovered one of the rarest trees in the world there, the Wollemi pine, a species so old that it has been found in the fossilized dung of dinosaurs—which is amazing to think of, considering how often the whole damn thing catches fire.

"Look on your left," says Greg. A copse of trees adjacent to the motorway has been reduced to black, ragged skeletons. We drive along for several miles, the burn straddling both sides of the highway, but I spot patches of green shoots already reappearing on the charred trunks. "They don't really get killed by a forest fire," explains Greg. "They start regrowing leaves almost immediately. It's amazing."

True to Greg's word, as we climb the Blue Mountains' plateau, the fog dissipates and blue skies emerge. After about an hour, we come to Echo Point, which overlooks an immense gorge, and we park the van and walk out to the observation platform. The gorge is some three kilometres across and perhaps a kilometre deep, and the steep, rosy-brown sandstone cliffs give way at their base to a dense carpet of forest. Now that the fog has lifted, the air in the valley takes on a definite violet hue, due to the oil droplets exuded by the eucalyptus.

By far the most interesting site, however, is the Three Sisters, an outlying ledge of sandstone that has been eroded into three scraggly, bulgy, scrub-covered pinnacles standing some eight hundred metres high. According to the Aborigine legend, three brothers from the Nepean tribe fell in love with three beautiful sisters—Meehni, Wimlah, and Gunnedoo—from the Katoomba tribe. Since tribal law forbade them marrying, the three brothers decided to elope with them, with or without their consent. When word of their plan got round, a Katoomba witch doctor turned the sisters into stone for their own safety. Unfortunately, he forgot to leave instructions for how to turn them back, and when he was killed in the subsequent melee, the three gals were locked for eternity in stone. That's why I always make sure the pharmacist keeps a copy of my prescription.

We motor on to the turnoff for the Jenolan Caves, which lie south, about fifty kilometres, at the base of the Krungle Bungles, which is one hell of a great name for a mountain range. The Jenolan Caves, discovered in 1838 by a convict bushranger, were carved out of limestone rock, over millions of years, by drippy groundwater. The latter is important because it gives nature a chance to form all kinds of interesting geological formations, like stalactites (stone icicles hanging from the roof), stalagmites (ditto, only from the floor), columns (when the two join together), and shawls (rippling flows, like aurora borealis in stone). Since the interior climate is cool and clammy, we don anoraks and long trousers, pay our entrance fee for the Lucas Cave, one of the main caverns within the Jenolan network, and head inside.

As a sport, most people rank spelunking right up there with home autopsy, but ever since I was first exposed to underground caverns as a lad, I have loved their deep, primal nature, not to mention the blatant Freudian overtones of it all. Of course, I don't recommend it for anyone who gets nervous in confined spaces. I discovered many years ago that miners have a foolproof way of determining claustrophobia.

As an undergraduate geologist, I spent one summer working in a nickel mine in Northern Ontario. On the first day, they outfitted fellow-undergraduate John and me with coveralls, tool belts, and electric lanterns that attached to the crown of our hard hats. The foreman escorted us deep into the dark realm below, then a half kilometre farther along a side tunnel, until we came to a rude wooden bench.

"There's a thousand-foot drop just ahead, so sit here and don't move," he commanded. "I'll be back to pick you up later."

We dutifully sat down and glanced around at our surroundings. The tunnel was perhaps three metres wide and two metres tall, big enough to allow a diesel scoop-tram to carry loads of ore from the seam to the crusher. The walls, carved from granite, were black with soot and blasting powder. Somewhere in the distance I could hear water dripping. I was about to ask if John wanted to come along to look at the thousand-foot drop, when I noticed my light beginning to flicker. Unbeknownst to us, the batteries we had been given were old and could only hold a charge for about an hour. Both lights went out, plunging us into complete blackness.

Now, there's the blackness of a dark cellar, and there's the blackness of a moonless night, but the blackness of a mine shaft under a thousand metres of solid granite is so complete that you can actually feel it sucking something out of the air.

"What should we do?" asked John.

"We sit here until he comes back," I said.

"That could be hours."

I tried not to think about that. Instead, we concentrated on using the faculties that weren't affected by the dark. Far off in the distance, toward the thousand-foot drop, I could hear the occasional *clack-*

clack as a rock plunged through the abyss. John pointed out the cool, unmistakable breeze emanating from the left, evidence that the air circulation was functioning. I could smell the stench of cordite, used to set off the blasting powder. We agreed it was amazing how much we relied on our sense of sight when there was so much other amazing stimulation in the world. Our astonishment lasted for about three minutes, then we took turns crying.

After what seemed like two hours, but was probably only twenty minutes, we saw a bobbing light approaching down the tunnel. The foreman soon appeared, clutching two new lanterns in his hands. Before he handed them to us, however, he ordered us to stand up and turn around. After a brief pirouette, he gruffly gave us the lanterns and took us to meet our supervisor, Boom-Boom Slanofski.

After the foreman departed, we told him that our lights had failed. Boom-Boom only laughed. "The supervisor does that to every newbie to check for claustrophobia."

"How can he tell?" I asked.

"Easy," said Boom-Boom. "If you pee your pants, you've got it."

All visitors to the Jenolan Caves have to be accompanied by a guide, which is just as well, because in order to reach the best part of the Lucas Cave, you have to descend a thirty-metre metal ladder, which is greasy with sweat. I don't have any problems with claustrophobia, having survived the bladder test in the underground mine, but I'm no big fan of plunging ten storeys.

"Is it safe?" I ask.

"No worries, mate," says Frank the guide. "You're as safe as houses." Considering how many homes were destroyed by fire only a few weeks ago, I take this news skeptically. Taking a tight grip on the rungs, I descend as carefully as possible.

The trip is worth it. Conservationists have done an excellent job of lighting the cave to reveal its splendours. We all exclaim in wonder at the immense columns and shawls, their colours ranging from pure white to deep ochre. Most of the features are railed off because, although they're made of stone, it is a very soft calcite, and even a casual brush with a bare hand leaves a mark that eventually turns black. Considering that 250,000 people visit the caves on an annual basis, even the most transitory contact would eventually ruin them.

I am staring at a stalactite high over my head, when I hear a distinctive peep echoing somewhere in the darkness. "What was that?"

Greg glances around in alarm. "It sounds like the Blue Mountain Water Skink."

Oh, good. "It's harmless, right?"

"About as harmless as a cross between a skunk and a crocodile can be."

I clear a sudden bout of phlegm from my throat. "What does it do?"

"Hits you with a paralyzing spray, then chews you up at leisure."

Frank the guide, who is hovering nearby, takes pity. "A skink's just a big gecko," he assures me. "But it's too cold down here for reptiles." He points a light toward the ceiling. "What you heard is a bat."

Everyone glances bat-ward, and I take the opportunity to strategically readjust my underpants. I spend the rest of the tour glancing nervously over my shoulder, nonetheless. After an hourlong tour, we climb back up the ladder into the great outdoors. The air is fresh and clean, and the warm sun beats down on the brilliant green ferns surrounding the entrance. Best of all, there isn't a skink in sight. ■

CHAPTER 8

Some Mighty Fine Wine

I am gently bidden awake early in the morning, not to the sound of waves crashing rhythmically against the nearby shore, but by car alarms. For some reason unfathomable to me, Australians set their alarm sensitivity so high that if a butterfly decides to flap by within ten metres of the bumper, the car emits a *bee-dong* reminiscent of a Stasi police car. Right now, several alarms are uniting in a symphony that the dead would appreciate for its resuscitating quality. I arise and conduct a fervent search for something small, dense, and bricklike, to no avail. Sighing, I pull on my shorts and running shoes and head for the beach.

It is early February, which is either the end of summer or the beginning of fall, depending on which way the wind blows. Today, the wind is bearing due north, having originated on some great glacial lobe in Antarctica. I have been running for about two months now, and I have gotten over my initial desire to lie down in the shade after the first hundred metres and have reached the malevolent point where my body *craves* a run—I'm addicted. As I head into the wind, the sand dances along the beach, stinging my legs, and I curse my own stupidity for taking up such a lunatic sport. Shouldn't I have at least lost my spare tire by now?

I am thusly occupied by such thoughts when I turn off the beach and head up the Corso. As I pass Coles liquor store, which has an immense lime-green sign in the window announcing "Last Year's Vintage On Sale," I suddenly realize it is harvest time in Australia and am so distracted by this revelation that I promptly collide with a begonia planter. Rubbing my shin, I return home to tell Linda.

"Guess what?" I announce, as I enter our apartment.

Linda looks up from her coffee. "You need stitches?"

"No. Well, maybe. What I meant to say is that it's wine harvest time. We should go on a tour."

Linda thinks this an excellent idea and, after rubbing some ointment onto my shin, digs out our trusty travel guide. Unfortunately, all the major growing regions are too far to the south and require a plane ride to reach them, an option well out of our limited travel budget. The Hunter Valley, however, is about a hundred kilometres north of Sydney, and a quick phone call to the charmingly named Abbey Hermitage confirms that they have rooms at a reasonable rate. We book a room for the following weekend and then sit down to work out how to get there.

"No worries," I explain. "We'll go to Lucky Luke's."

Lucky Luke's, an independent car-rental agency, is a few blocks west of us on Pittwater Road and consists of a small shack in an asphalt lot, surrounded by a fence topped with barbed wire. Considering the rather motley collection of cars in the lot, the barbed wire is a bit of overkill, but perhaps car thieves are a demented lot hereabouts, which might explain the hyperactive car alarms. A sign on the fence announces "Nobody Beets Our Prices."

We are greeted by the owner, a man in blue coveralls, covered with splotches of oil. Luke was once perhaps six feet tall, but some sort of spinal trauma has left him bent over almost double. We gaze down into a roundish face that looks as though it has passed through a windscreen at high speed, and I begin to suspect where the "Lucky" part comes in. We introduce ourselves and explain that we would like to go on a wine tour of the Hunter Valley for the weekend. "I'm looking for something cheap and reliable to rent," I say.

"I've got just the ticket." Lucky leads us over to a white Holden SB sedan. "I can let you have this one for twenty-five dollars a day."

I whistle in appreciation. That's about half the price that the major car-rental agencies are charging. "How come it's so cheap?"

Lucky glances conspiratorially in both directions, then whispers his explanation. "They're all wrecks. I buy 'em cheap and fix 'em up."

"Is it safe?" asks Linda.

"There's a man who owns a motel just around the corner," responds Lucky. "Whenever he needs to rent a car for his wife, he asks specifically for this one."

I resist the temptation to ask if he's referring to Gabor, our beleaguered Hungarian friend back at the Budapest. I walk around the car and check the interior and under the hood—Lucky seems to have done a fine job of reinstalling things like tires and motors in the right spots. We agree to hire the car and make arrangements to pick it up on Friday.

When we return home, an ambulance is parked in front of the Seaview. At first, I scan the beach, assuming someone is in need of resuscitation, but the doors of the apartment open and two EMS technicians emerge with a stretcher, upon which rests a small form. Her face is covered by an oxygen mask, but there's no mistaking the bluish hair that fringes it. I wait until Gertrude is loaded into the back of the vehicle before approaching the driver.

"I'm her neighbour next door. Can you tell me what happened?"

"Had a bit of a fall," he explains.

"Will she be all right?"

"Looks like a crack on the old noggin and a sprained arm. Good thing she was able to reach the phone." He shakes his head. "Old folks shouldn't be living on their own." He climbs into the cab and leans out the window. "Had one old doll fall and bang her head on the sink." He glances over his shoulder, then lowers his voice. "Neighbours finally had the fire department break in a week later—couldn't stand the yammering of her dog. Not a pretty sight." The ambulance pulls away, siren wailing.

Later that evening, Gertrude's son Kevin brings her back from the hospital. I can hear them in the hallway—him pleading for her to come to his place for a few days until she is better, and her pooh-poohing the idea, reassuring him that she is just fine. After he leaves, I brew some tea and go over and knock on her door. Gertrude opens it and lets me in. Her wrist is wrapped and her arm is in a sling, and a patch of gauze is taped to her forehead.

"Care for a spot of tea?" I ask.

"That would be lovely."

While I fetch some cups from the kitchen, Gertrude settles back into her stuffed rocking chair in front of the television. Her crochet needles rest on a side table. She ignores them, staring straight ahead, a sad, defeated look on her face. I bring her a cup and sit on the settee nearby. "Mind telling me what happened?"

Gertrude points to a nearby window. "The curtain came off its runner. I fell off a chair while trying to hook it back up—I don't know what's wrong, I've done it a hundred times before."

I glance over at the window; the curtain's still off the track. I pull out a chair and climb up, adjusting it so it once again slides smoothly. I get down and put the chair back at the kitchen table. "Gertrude, if there's ever anything you need to do around the house, you know, moving heavy stuff or climbing on chairs, you come and get me. I'll be glad to help."

"Thanks, love. I'll be all right."

A few days later, on a fine Thursday evening, Greg and I are wandering the Corso. Greg has finished his courier work for the day and has come to Manly to look for a place to open his coffee shop.

We stop in front of Pinocchio's Restaurant. "This would be perfect," he says. "You're far enough off the Corso that you're not paying high rents, but close enough to get all the walk-by traffic."

I point to a number of commercial buildings that sit across the street. "You'd probably get a lot of office workers coming in for coffee break and lunch, as well."

Greg stares at the restaurant. "Too bad it's already occupied."

I recall Pinocchio's Hairburger Special. "No worries, mate. I have a feeling it won't be long before it's vacant again."

We walk back along the Corso to the Bristol Hotel and order a pint. Sitting out on the balcony, I recount Gertrude's accident. "What I can't figure out is why she doesn't go back to her son's place for a few days."

Greg sips his beer. "She doesn't want to lose her freedom."

"What?"

"You ever hear the national anthem of Australia?"

As a matter of fact, I have. I fell asleep the other night in front of the TV, and when I woke up, they were playing this god-awful song. "I think it's called 'Advance Australia Fair.'"

"No, the *real* national anthem—'Waltzing Matilda.'"

"Sure, I've heard that, too."

"But do you know what it's about?"

"Can't say as I do."

Greg recites the lyrics, thankfully, without singing:

Once a jolly swagman camped by a billabong,
Under the shade of a coolibah-tree,
And he sang as he watched and waited till his billy boiled,
"Who'll come a-waltzing Matilda with me?"

Down came a jumbuck to drink at the billabong:
Up jumped the swagman and grabbed him with glee.
And he sang as he shoved that jumbuck in his tucker-bag,
"You'll come a-waltzing Matilda with me."

Up rode a squatter, mounted on his thoroughbred;
Down came the troopers, one, two, three:
"Who's that jolly jumbuck you've got in your tucker-bag?
You'll come a-waltzing Matilda with me!"

Up jumped the swagman and sprang into the billabong;
"You'll never catch me alive!" said he;
And his ghost may be heard as you pass by that billabong,
"You'll come a-waltzing Matilda with me!"

The words are strange, and I admit as much. "I don't understand it."

"It was written by an Australian poet, Banjo Paterson. It's about a swagman, a bush hobo, who steals a sheep and gets caught by the police. But rather than go to jail, he jumps into a nearby pond and drowns."

"He'd rather kill himself than lose his freedom?"

Greg sips his beer, then nods. "We're a funny lot that way."

It has taken several months to decompress, even with our sojourn in the Cooks, but I have finally reached the point where I consider myself a true Ozzie. Although I cannot surf, or play Aussie Rules Football, or even down a can of lager in less than ten seconds without it scooting back out my nose, I have learned how to spend a day entirely in pursuit of pointless leisure and, thus, have achieved Australian nirvana.

Arising at an hour sufficiently late in the morning to preclude any of the neighbours from thinking I might be pursuing an occupation even vaguely honest, I brew a cup of coffee and prepare a bowl of cereal, with fresh fruit and whole milk, to fortify myself for the coming day. After breakfast, I check my diary. First on the list of duties is changing into my swimsuit, donning a pair of sunglasses, tucking the morning newspaper under my arm, and trundling down to the beach to catch up on world affairs. This can take several hours, especially if the need for a refreshing nap between the Local News and Arts & Leisure sections arises. Generally, however, I finish in time to return to the apartment and freshen up with a shower, in preparation for shopping for lunch. By now, the heart of the summer has passed, along with the fierce heat that can turn a stretch of road into a version of the La Brea Tar Pits. Still, old habits die hard, and as I make my way down a side street, I still pick out the shadiest part of the sidewalk, while moving along at flip-flop velocity, which is close to the speed attained by maple syrup in Québec in January.

Travelling at such terminal velocity gives you a chance to observe things closely, and I have to say that some of the architecture away from the Corso holds all the charm of a retired rugby linebacker in a latex thong. Most of the buildings along the beachfront are Costa Brava-style holiday apartments—huge, bulgy things, twenty storeys high and clad in orange stucco, with sweeping balconies and three storeys of car parks that hang their butt ends over the streets running behind. And that's the best part; a block in from the beach, it gets even more decrepit, with row after row of cinder-block retail malls and rundown clapboard homes waiting for a facelift, courtesy of the next cyclone. Were it not for the brilliant, unrelenting blue sky and the flower-bedecked trees growing on the curb, I might be offended.

There are several greengrocers in town, but I prefer the one run by a Greek family near the ferry marina. They always have lots of fresh papayas, melons, and mangoes to make fruit salad, as well as a wide selection of lettuce, tomatoes, and sundry vegetables. Mostly though, they let me pick and poke at things and taste the grapes without getting their ear hairs in a knot. A nearby deli makes an appetizing Black Forest ham and Gruyère cheese sandwich, with pickles, mayo, and mustard, on a thick, crunchy roll.

After lunch, I get down to work on my laptop computer. Since arriving in Manly, I have devoted an hour or two each afternoon to my novel, a mystery thriller set in fifteenth-century France in the castle of Vincennes, outside of Paris. I call it *Magnus the Magnificent*. Someone is trying to poison Henry V, King of England and France, after his victory at the Battle of Agincourt. It's up to his faithful court jester, a dwarf named Magnus the Magnificent, to uncover the plotters. Could it be Gilles de Rais, the scheming emissary from the exiled King Charles VII? Or how about Isabella of Bavaria, the treacherous French queen deposed by Henry? Ooh, the list is endless.

I roll out a large sheet of paper, which organizes the intertwined subplots, then sit down and write a few pages of dialogue, essentially taking dictation from the characters. When I explain this to Linda, she recommends I spend less time in the sun, but it's true that you reach the point where they take on lives and independence, and if I try to force them to do something they don't want to do, they tell me.

Later in the afternoon, if we aren't playing squash or going to an aerobics class, Linda and I head for the library. Not only is it blissfully air conditioned, but there is also a huge collection of spy thrillers, murder mysteries, and general-mayhem books on tap for the modest price of membership. In addition, it has an excellent selection of CDs and tapes that we borrow and listen to on the ghetto blaster we bought at Payday, an upscale pawnshop on Steyne.

One thing I never do in Canada is watch TV, but here, we always reserve an hour in front of the boob tube toward the dinner hour. This is, without a doubt, the trashiest time to watch television anywhere in the world, and the Australian Broadcasting Corporation doesn't let us down. They show a lot of British comedies, including *Are You Being Served?* and *Keeping Up Appearances*, as well as that perennial favourite *Skippy the Bush Kangaroo*, which I recall watching as a child and wishing I could trade in my little sister for a jumpy pet like that.

We serve dinner on the balcony and, then, if we feel like a night out, go see a movie at the Manly Twin Cinemas. It doesn't seem to favour Richard Gere, which is unfortunate, but Mel Gibson seems quite popular hereabouts. Linda often compares me to Mel—at least in his role as Rocky in the animated feature movie *Chicken Run*. I take compliments wherever I find them. After the movie, we usually stroll down the Corso for a pint of lager at the Bristol and then return home along the promenade, watching the silvery luminescent sheen of waves crashing upon the beach. It's *hard yakka*, as the locals like to sarcastically note, but, hey, somebody's got to do it.

Friday arrives, and Linda and I show up at Lucky Luke's to pay our deposit and take possession of the car. On the drive back to the Seaview, I am pleasantly surprised to find that not only does the Holden SB possess an admirable set of brakes, but it has a little pep, as well.

We load our luggage and are soon following various roads through town, until we connect with the Sydney–Newcastle Freeway, a multi-lane motorway, heading north. As soon as we leave the city, I put the car on cruise control and settle back to enjoy the view. The freeway runs through several national parks, starting with Ku-ring-gai Chase and Muogamarra Nature Reserve. I admire the selection of wildlife resting on the side of the road—mostly, it would appear, small nocturnal marsupials with a fondness for headlights. On both sides of the motorway, the rolling hills have been denuded by the recent arsonist fires, exposing the orange granite beneath.

We have just crossed the large bridge that spans Hawkesbury River and are ascending into the hills of Brisbane Water National Park, when we approach a slow-moving semi-truck in the lane ahead. As I touch the brakes to slow down, a large portion of the dashboard separates from the rest of the car and ends up in my lap. Linda is able to hold it away from the gas and brake pedals, until I bring the car safely to a halt in a lay-by. I examine the chunk of plastic; the locking screws appear to have been improperly set and I crawl around under the dash until I have it in place again. We are too far down the road to return for another vehicle, but now I know what the SB stands for: "Shit Box." Cursing Lucky, we set off once again.

The rest of the drive is uneventful, in the sense that all vehicular components remain where they should. We pass Tuggerah

Lake and Lake Macquarie, huge brackish expanses of water adjacent to the Pacific shore, before turning westward inland. The flat fields near the coast soon give way to pasture land, as we enter the high country surrounding our destination. The Hunter Valley is located east of the Broken Back Range, an ancient, weathered ridge of basalt. It sits in a broad, rolling valley that is cut by shallow streambeds and sprinkled with knots of scrubby trees, where the soil has proven too infertile for cultivation.

You wouldn't immediately think of the Hunter Valley as ideal for wine growing. The farthest from the equator of any of Australia's wine-growing regions, at thirty-three degrees south, it suffers from a dry spring, which can inhibit blossoms, and a hot, humid fall, which can turn a fine wine grape into jam fodder in no time. But since the dawn of European settlement in the 1820s, pioneers such as the Tyrrell and Wyndham families have planted a wide variety of grapes in the region, experimenting to find the best combination of grape type and geography.

We pass through Cessnock, the largest town in the region, and continue toward the village of Pokolbin, in the heart of the vineyards. A road sign for the Abbey Hermitage directs us to our turnoff. The private lane is lined on both sides with old oak barrels that have been cut in half and planted with geraniums and petunias, and we follow the floral honour guard for several hundred metres through a vineyard, the grapes hanging thick and full. I am half expecting a medieval retreat, but the hotel is a traditional Australian station, a low building built of white-painted wood and covered in a gleaming tin roof, which extends out to form a long veranda, supported by wooden posts.

We park beside a door marked "Office" and, inside, find a roundish woman, with curly blonde hair and sunburned cheeks, sitting behind the registration desk. Vera and her husband, Ben, native Australians, own the hotel and, after signing us in, she directs us to our room on the west side of the building. The large and spacious room has patio doors facing the Broken Back Range, plaster walls painted white, and an electric fan fixed to the open-beamed ceiling, some three and a half metres above us. Throw rugs break up the cool terra-cotta floor tiles. I am relieved to see that there is nary a bush-fire painting in sight—the walls are decorated with watercolours of various vinous scenes of harvesting, crushing, and copious imbibing. Taking the hint, we hop back into the sb and head off for a tasting.

The nearest vineyard happens to be Tyrrell's, whose wine has always been a personal favourite of mine. They have a way of making big, full-bodied reds that go well with barbecued steak and lamb and are also very adept at thick, creamy Chardonnays that roll about on the palate, giving off a series of flavours that start with peaches and end with butterscotch. Our guide is Emily, a young woman with thick, auburn hair, who leads us through ancient cellars, where oaken casks rest in cool darkness. Actually, the earthy touch is mostly patina, as the winery boasts all the modern machinery and equipment of a major international exporter.

After the tour of shining steel tanks and bottling assembly lines, we retire to the tasting room, where the real fun begins. Emily pours various samplers, and we work our way through a series of whites and reds. Bruce the vintner, a sunburned native of the valley, complete with wide-brimmed hat and khaki shorts, is more than happy to explain which grapes do well, and where. He says the black, silty loam of the valley is well suited to the Sémillon grape, which produces a rich, honeyed white when aged for a year in French white oak and then left for over a decade to mature in the bottle. Chardonnay, under a similar regime, is also quite popular in the region. As for reds, although Cabernet Sauvignon and Merlot are grown throughout the district, the most popular red by far is the Shiraz grape, which produces a rich, complex wine that takes decades and decades to mature, kind of like me.

I must say, I am impressed with our first exposure to the

Australian wine industry. Linda and I have toured wineries in France and California, and we have found that Americans and Europeans tend to look down their noses at Down Under wines. However, not only is the knowledge and experience of the vintners, the sophistication of the processing, and the quality of the wine comparable, but I also find the total lack of elitism as refreshing as a crisp, cold rosé on a hot summer day.

I'm sure Bruce would have happily stood around for hours answering our questions, but it was time to continue our journey. Over the course of the afternoon, we visit several more vineyards, before finally heading back to the Abbey Hermitage, the trunk of the SB filled with wine. During our tour, Vera and Ben have been busy preparing supper, and we arrive to discover a delicious smell wafting on the evening breeze. I wander over to check, but Ben won't let me peek under the barbecue cover. "It's a surprise," he explains.

As I am recounting our afternoon's wine tasting to Ben, I notice a pack of dogs weaving in and out of the vineyards, sniffing the ground. "What are they hunting after?"

"Wallabies," explains Ben. "They like to nibble the grapes."

After a sherry cocktail in the bar, Linda and I and a half-dozen other guests are escorted out to an arbour, where several tables are covered with white-linen cloths and decorated with candles. Ben's dogs have returned from the vineyard and are obediently lying near their master's barbecue. As the last magenta glow of dusk disappears behind the serrated, charcoal-blue silhouette of the Broken Back Range, we are served a delicious platter of peppers roasted in balsamic vinegar and olive oil, baby potatoes in butter and parsley, and rack of lamb. Or at least I think it was lamb; the way those dogs were eyeing our meal, I have my doubts.

It is almost the middle of February. We have been in Australia for more than five months, and our six-month visas will soon expire. Taking a lesson from our experience in the Cook Islands, I don't intend to let them lapse. Even though we have to leave the country to renew our visas, that shouldn't be a problem—our airline tickets take us to Auckland, New Zealand, where we can update them. The question is, do we move on or do we return to Australia?

One morning over coffee, Linda and I sit down and talk about it. "Do you like it here?" I ask Linda.

"I love it. The weather is beautiful, the people are wonderful, and I've never felt happier in my entire life." Linda has reached her goal of losing ten pounds and looks lovely and svelte. "I could stay here forever."

"Me, too. For the first time in my life, I've had time to pursue writing for the pure joy of creating something, and I love it. But what would we do for a living?"

"We don't need a lot of money to get by." Linda points to my almost-completed manuscript. "You can write, and I can get work as an instructor at an aerobics club." I give Linda a hug, and she seals it with a kiss. It's a deal, then.

A few days later, the phone rings. At my request, Greg has checked around and found the name of a lawyer who specializes in immigration. "Is he any good?" I ask.

"He's cheap, and that's what counts," says Greg.

A few days later, we take the ferry to Circular Quay and seek out Havisham & Havisham, Attorneys at Law, in downtown Sydney. Their office is in a six-storey brick building that has seen better days; the elevator wheezes and clatters to the top floor.

Havisham, either the former or the latter, is dressed in a three-piece suit of pinstriped, blue wool. His face, puffy and clean shaven, pokes out of his collar like a white balloon. He rises briefly from the chair behind his desk to shake our hands, then settles down to business.

"First, let's attend to the formalities," he announces. "Do you have the fifty dollars?"

"Cash or cheque?" I ask.

"Cash, of course." I hand the bills across the desk, and he tucks them into his vest pocket. "Now, what is it you wish to do?"

"We'd like to immigrate to Australia."

"The easiest way is if you have a sponsor offering you a job."

"Sorry, no job prospects," says Linda. "Is there another way to qualify?"

Havisham pulls out a clipboard from his desk. "We use a point system here. Let's see how you do." He rattles off questions about our age, occupation, education, and several other background details, then stops and tallies our scores. "*Hmnn*," he mutters.

"What's wrong?" I ask.

Havisham shakes his head. "I'm afraid you don't qualify on merit. You're too old, for one thing, and if there's anything we don't need, it's more writers."

"Does this mean we can't immigrate?"

"Not necessarily. You *are* from Canada."

"They favour people from the Commonwealth?"

Havisham glances at the ceiling. "Let's just say that they don't eat much curry there." He pats the vest pocket where he tucked the fifty dollars. "Perhaps, with a little help, we can turn that to your advantage."

"I see." I glance at Linda, who, like me, is at a loss for words, and we stand and take our leave. We remain silent until we are out of the building and standing in the sunshine, free of his presence. I turn to Linda. "Did he mean that, because we are white, we can buy our way to the head of the line?"

Linda shakes her head. "I don't know, but if that's what it takes, then I don't want to do it."

"Me either." We head back to Manly, sadder but wiser.

The next day, I call the airline and book our flight to Auckland.

"I don't want to go," says Linda.

"I don't either, but it's time we moved on. Maybe we'll love New Zealand as much as Manly."

In one way, we are fortunate—we haven't accumulated nearly as much crap as we had in Calgary. Not that we wouldn't have, if given the opportunity to replace our beige overstuffed furniture with something that didn't smell of fish, but lack of time and, mostly, money has kept our belongings down to a few posters, the ghetto blaster, and a rather dented pasta pot that Greg donated to our cause. We decide that the ghetto blaster and pasta pot will be just the ticket while cruising the back roads of New Zealand. The posters, on the other hand, won't do much to posh up a rental car and we reluctantly leave them behind for the next tenant to use to cover up the beer hole.

We book the first part of our journey to Auckland and inform Greg, who promptly decides that a going-away party at our house on the eve of our departure would be ideal. This, he explains, is the traditional Oz way of ridding the home of unwanted alcoholic beverages and snacks.

Gertrude drops in to say goodbye. By now, she has fully recovered, but I still insist on visiting her every week or so to see if she needs anything done. I suspect she humours me by putting in burnt-out light bulbs just so I can change them. Linda brews a cup of tea and we all sit on our balcony. Gertrude gazes far over the ocean, eastwards. "You know, I've never been to Canada. I'd love to come and see it some day."

Linda gives her a hug. "You can come and visit us and stay as long as you want."

When she leaves, Gertrude gives us a box of Turkish candy and a kiss on the cheek; she smells of lavender talcum powder. "Thank you for being wonderful neighbours," she says.

When I tell Señora Fortado at the chuck shop that we are leaving in a few days, she waves a finger at me. "You are a lucky man to have such a beautiful wife. You take care of her." I promise to do that, and she packs two extra cobs of corn into our meal as a parting gift.

When I drop off some papers to our rental agency, old man Redding is out, but Malcolm is in residence, his feet on the sofa and his nose buried deeply in a stack of surf-fishing magazines. He is delighted when I tell him that he is welcome to the fillets of some mysterious ocean dweller left in our freezer by the previous tenant and avidly wishes us a safe journey.

Our farewell party unfolds in uncharacteristically docile fashion, with guests limiting themselves to throwing nothing more than a few random whoops off the balcony. My appetizer, pork ribs in Gord's secret sauce, is met with universal approval, and the tufty beige material on the sofa proves to be perfect for cleaning sticky fingers. We manage to put a major dent in the keg of Foster's sitting in a large tub of ice, and several vintages of bladder wine are sacrificed to Bacchus. Nobody *chunders* in the stairwell, even though I am told it is a traditional Oz salutation of farewell.

Alex and Jenny must leave early to rescue their babysitter, but Greg and Heather stick it out until early morning. Greg and I greet the first glimmer of dawn over the Pacific Ocean as the last of a well-aged bottle of Shiraz from the Hunter Valley drains into our glasses. "I've got something for you," I say. I go into the apartment and fetch out a box.

"What is it?"

"My novel; I finished it. I wanted you to have a copy."

"Brilliant. I've brought a little going-away prezzie for you, as well." From his rucksack, he pulls out his copy of *Thailand: The Beautiful Cookbook*, which I had admired during our first dinner months ago.

"What a wonderful gift—you shouldn't have," I say.

"No worries, mate. I got a new one at the wedding."

Clutching the book under one arm, I swing the other in a rather graceless arc that encompasses the beach, the Norfolk pines, our apartment, and several pieces of rust from the balcony railing. "I'm going to miss you and all this."

"I'm not going to miss you," says Greg.

"You're not?"

"Nope. You're going to be back before I have a chance to."

What *will* I miss of Australia? The pints of lager on the balcony of the Bristol Hotel under a full moon; the scent of eucalyptus oil hanging in the air of the Blue Mountains; the Sydney Opera House by night; riding the *JetCat*; eating barbecued shrimp.

I regret that I've seen only a tiny portion of Australia. I would have loved to visit the Great Barrier Reef, and Cairns and Perth and Adelaide, and a host of other places. Not Ayers Rock, mind you—I can't think of anything more pointless than driving six days across a vast, lifeless desert to glimpse the world's biggest bloody pebble. I am very sorry, however, that I didn't see a little penguin or observe a funnel spider, and I regret even more that I never watched a saltwater crocodile glide malevolently out of the water and snag a riverboat pilot, his screams of "*rippah*" echoing across the water as he is dragged to his doom.

But these are small things. On the other hand, I am immensely happy at having forgone another endless Canadian winter, instead, basking on a beautiful beach full of topless Australians. I am delighted not only to have spent time with old friends like Greg, but also to have made new friends like Alex and Jenny and Gertrude. I am especially proud of the mystery novel I have written here, which the unfailingly objective Linda tells me is very good.

As our plane lifts off and wings out over the ocean, I stare back at the receding shore. My heart longs to remain in Australia; we have experienced great happiness in Manly and are very sad to leave. But, sometimes fate takes a hand in these things, and we have learned to go with the flow rather than fight it. New adventures await in New Zealand. ■

Tasman Sea

North Island

•Auckland

Lake
Taupo

•Taupo

Tongariro
National Park

•Napier

Taradale•

Nelson
Neudorf • Picton
•Westport

•Wellington

•Franz Josef

•Christchurch
•Akaroa

•Haast

Pacific Ocean

•Wanaka
•Queenstown

South Island

Stewart
Island

•Half Moon
 Bay

N

W   E

S

NEW ZEALAND

⊢━━━┤ = 150 km

CHAPTER 9

Auckland Ahoy

It is a three-hour flight from Australia to New Zealand, and by early afternoon, our destination appears on the horizon. The North Island of New Zealand stretches in an emerald arc of cone-shaped mountains, interspersed with green, undulating hills. Auckland itself is sandwiched into a narrow, snaking isthmus, some eight kilometres wide and twenty-five kilometres long, and is bounded by two immense harbours, Waitemata and Manukau.

Our plane heads directly toward the international airport south of the city and swings low over the aquamarine waters of Manukau Harbour, before touching down on the runway. We retrieve our baggage and discover that my pasta pot has been used by the Sydney Airport bowling league for target practice, but fortunately, the ghetto blaster seems to have survived.

After the customs agent gives my now rather battered belongings a perfunctory glare, we are ejected into New Zealand proper, where we are met by Morton, a Maori lad sent to pick us up by our car-rental agency. Morton, who is wearing a black Stetson, proves to be one of the most taciturn people we have met on our trip. Perhaps he's channelling Gary Cooper beneath his hat, or maybe on the weekend he's a tour guide for zombies. Either way, we drive for perhaps ten minutes in perfect silence, until we come to A2Z Rental Cars.

Nell, the daughter of the family who owns the business, takes our details and fills out the forms. She escorts us out to the yard, where we pick up our chariot for the next six weeks: a white, four-door Toyota sedan.

"I hope you don't mind bright colours," she apologizes. I glance inside, where the interior is upholstered in yellow fabric. Some people might be appalled, but I find it kind of charming. Besides, it is virtually theft-proof—who'd want it? We promptly christen it the Egg, pile our worldly belongings inside, and head for Auckland.

As far as cities go, Auckland is virtually brand new. When Captain James Cook passed this way in 1769, he didn't even bother to enter the harbour. It wasn't until peace was established in 1840 that the Maori nations invited the British to settle in the region, and Lieutenant-Governor William Gibson named the new capital after his naval commander, Lord Auckland. Two years later, five hundred Scottish settlers were plopped onto the fertile ground and began fertilizing what is now a city of 1.3 million souls, all living in bungalows surrounded by large lawns and verdant shrubbery.

We follow the Southern Motorway into town and find our motel, which is near the city centre. After checking in, we wander down to the harbour, where tall ships dot the quays and sailboats churn the waters. The downtown core is a mix of nineteenth-century sandstone façades and high-rises clad in mirrored glass. Several interesting shops on Queen Street beckon, but it is now late afternoon, and we decide that a round of liquid refreshments is more appropriate. We pop into a bistro on Anzac Avenue, decorated in early camp, with photos of Marilyn Monroe and Marlene Dietrich dotting the walls, amid chintz fabric and perfect little Tiffany lamps. We opt for the patio.

Our waiter appears with a wine list and a pointy, silver spike about five centimetres long jutting from his lower lip. I am immediately intrigued as to how he prevents ale from dripping down his chin while sipping a pint, but can't think of a sufficiently casual way of bringing it up in conversation, other than leaning over and flicking the damn thing. He makes a suggestion regarding the day's special wine, and I quickly agree to two glasses. By the time he returns, at Linda's insistence, I am sitting on my hands and thus able to resist temptation long enough to inquire about the wine's provenance.

"It's a Sauvignon Blanc, grown in Marlborough Sounds on the South Island," he explains. Normally, I'm not a big fan of this particular grape, finding it generally thin and vinegary, but this is an absolutely joyous vintage, thick and well balanced, framing the trademark flintiness that aficionados look for in this variety. We order another round, settle back, and observe our surroundings.

It is the beginning of fall and the local citizenry are celebrating in traditional fashion, with a gay parade. Now, Sydney's gay parade down in Kings Cross may be more famous, but what Aucklanders lack in profile, they more than make up for in fervour. An assemblage of men in pink tutus and brightly coloured feather headgear sashays down Anzac Avenue, right past the bistro. One, a little loose in the G-string, is doing some advertising for friendship; obviously, it's a swinging town. I turn and ask the waiter where they are heading, and he eyes the passing throng longingly. "Karangahape Road. It's the gay red light district." Ah, Kiwi studs for rent—there's a concept to warm your cockles. I didn't notice the district on my official tour map, but I guess it was an oversight.

We finish our drinks and return to our motel to change into our running gear. We head toward the Auckland Domain, an open area of vast lawns and large trees, which, according to my map, includes a volcano crater in which concerts are held. I am thinking it would be an excellent venue for Kenny G, but all we see is a few brightly coloured men, who seem to have wandered from the parade in the direction of the thick shrubbery.

We return to the hotel to wash up, before heading back to the bistro we've dubbed Chez Chintz to once again take up residence on the patio overlooking the street. We order *Moules à l'Ardennaise*, fresh New Zealand bivalves steamed in a mixture of butter, cream, sautéed onions, and fried bacon, a dish that goes extremely well with Marlborough Sauvignon Blanc, which we have decided is our house wine. After dinner, we consider walking down toward the harbour to enjoy the night scene, but we have just spent the last several months in a large, vibrant city, and whatever charms Auckland holds, our hearts are not in the bright lights, red or otherwise, and we soon return home and prepare to venture forth into the heartland of New Zealand.

The next day dawns sunny, bright, and warm. After a brunch of coffee and toast with Vegemite, which, as near as I can tell, is tar flavoured with peanut butter, we fire up the Egg and head south. After several kilometres of manicured lawns, suburban Auckland gives way to farmland dotted with lakes, the odd cinder cone, and lots and lots of fluffy sheep. We are on our way to Taupo, some two hundred kilometres away, and meander through places like Hamilton, Bombay, and Ngaruawahia, where we have to stop to let me unroll my tongue after I try to pronounce the town's welcome sign aloud. We notice that many of the natives grin and wave in our general direction, a spontaneous reaction, no doubt, to the sight of our car's upholstery.

We are a few kilometres north of our destination when I spot a sign announcing Geyserland. "Let's stop and check out it out," I say. There are many jurisdictions in North America where this is grounds for justifiable homicide, but Linda and I had a mutual agreement written into our wedding vows in which I get one geological attraction a month, in return for unlimited access to shoe stores. I recommend this arrangement to all men who wish to see the other side of forty.

We pull down a side road and stop at the entrance, a series of rustic wooden buildings housing the souvenir shop. Geyserland is adjacent to a small lake, surrounded by forest-covered hills. At various points around the lake, white limestone precipitate tumbles down to the shore, creating frozen cascades of rock, and when I step outside the car, my lungs are instantly filled with the pungent smell of sulphur. Does it get any better than this?

We pay our entrance fee and set off on a self-directed tour around a carefully marked path. Our first stop is the Soda Fountain, a roiling pond of extremely hot water emanating from a pit in the middle of a tropical glade. Next on the agenda is the Boiling Mud Pit, a mass of grey ooze that periodically emits bubbly farts of sulphur. A sign adjacent to the attraction warns you not to enter the pit, which I consider excellent advice. We stop to admire several more thermal features, although I pass on Aladdin's Cave, a large cavern carved into the hillside by the dissolution of its limestone core—I still have an issue with skinks. For her part, Linda enjoys the excursion. It is a chance to get out of the car and stretch her legs, as well as wear a little leather off the soles. I envision a new pair of Charles Jourdan pumps in the near future.

We head back to the car and continue on to the town of Taupo, which is adjacent to the lake of the same name. The circular body of water, some twenty-five kilometres in diameter, was created thirty-six thousand years ago by an immense volcanic explosion that ejected an estimated eight hundred cubic kilometres of rock and ash into the atmosphere. To give you an idea of the relative size of the explosion, Mount St. Helens, which covered much of western North America with ash in 1980, only spewed around one cubic kilometre. The explosion at Taupo was so violent that the volcano completely disappeared, leaving behind the sunken caldera and a new lake. According to the geological record, the vast plume of magma that still exists beneath Lake Taupo erupts periodically; the last one, some eighteen hundred years ago, barbecued everything for twenty thousand square kilometres around, and the next one could happen any time.

The Lakeview Motel is located on the edge of Taupo. Kiwis love to travel their island nation by car, cycle, and thumb, so countless cinder-block motels capped with tin roofs dot the landscape. The Lakeview, the archetypal example, is a low, single-storey building, stretching some sixty metres, with twenty-four rooms, a dozen to each side. It is painted a grey-beige colour, reminiscent of the mud pits in Geyserland.

Considering the geological time bomb beneath our feet, I expect the owner of the Lakeview to be a tad on the nervous side. When we pull into the motel's parking lot, however, Ross is resting beside the pool, in an aluminum folding chair, drinking a can of ale, and generally regarding life in a languid manner. He is tall and lanky and the proud owner of a nose the size of *Webster's Thesaurus*. He rises from the chair long enough to fetch a key to our room, then returns to his existential musings by the pool, his beer well shaded from the sun.

Our room features the same cinder-block walls as those found on the exterior, although they are painted a more cheerful yellow-beige. The furniture is worn to the point where the fabric shines a dull grey, and the dishes and pots in the kitchen show signs of abuse so spectacular that I can only conclude that the Lakeview is the motel of choice for vacationing baggage handlers.

The decor calls out a single message: get the hell out of here and see something.

The town of Taupo, laid out in grid fashion, is bounded by hills to the north, south, and east, and by the lake to the west. We walk the half kilometre into town, which I reckon contains several thousand souls whose primary occupation seems to be waiting for the next Big One. A cadre of mostly senior citizens is parked on lakeside benches, staring out at the water, alert for the first wisp of impending doom.

We forgo this particular pastime in favour of shopping for dinner. A supermarket at one end of the main drag beckons with large posters promising a wide range of unbelievable savings. Linda is interested in cooking spaghetti with meat sauce, but I feel more venturesome. "Let's see if we can find something unique to New Zealand," I suggest.

We head over to the frozen-food section, which contains a large selection of meat and fish, but nothing truly exotic. I am beginning to despair when I spot a small, brown object the size of a bowling ball, which the sticker on its side identifies as mutton bird.

"Maybe it's a cross between sheep and chicken," offers Linda.

I hoist it from the freezer to inspect it more closely. The printing on the freezer wrap informs me that this particular delicacy is found only on some isolated outcrops of land at the very southern tip of New Zealand. It is strangely uninformative regarding preparation technique, however. "I wonder how you cook it?"

A Maori man shopping in the aisle stops to explain. "It's easy. You put the mutton bird and a large rock into a big pot of water and boil them for three days—then you throw out the mutton bird and eat the rock!" I thank him for this information and chuck the bird back in the freezer.

Spaghetti and meat sauce doesn't sound so bad, after all.

The following morning I arise early. It is another brilliant day, the sky a clear blue and the clean smell of the lake carrying in the breeze. Outside our room, a group of songbirds is gathered in the bushes surrounding the motel, their chirping carrying in through the kitchen window. I am up early because I want to surprise Linda with a cup of coffee in bed. The coffee perk consists of a small aluminum pot, with a spout on one side, and a lid with a transparent glass knob. Inside is a tiny basket on stilts. The evening before, I had asked Ross how it worked.

"You just fill the basket with coffee and the pot with water and stick it on the stove," he explained. "It's *drongo*-proof."

"What?"

"Even an *idjit* can do it."

Thus heartened, I fill the device to the brim, plop it on the stovetop, and turn it on high. Just then, a brilliant flash of feathery colour passes the kitchen window—it is a rainbow lorikeet, just like the one at Alex and Jenny's home in Garigal—as it heads for a rhododendron bush covered with bright red flowers. Grabbing my camera, I scurry outside, and much to my delight, it remains in the yard, darting in and out of the bush.

I try to get a picture but am distracted by an odious noise, somewhere between a belch and puking. I am half expecting the momentary eruption of Taupo, but when I glance over my shoulder, I spot instead a fountain of brown liquid arcing through our kitchen window onto the lawn. I rush back inside to find the coffee percolator doing its impersonation of *The Exorcist*, sporadically spewing a mix of grounds and boiling mud over the stove, wall, and floor. I kill the gas burner and, using an oven mitt, transfer the offending appliance to the sink, where it gurgles and heaves malevolently for several minutes.

Linda calls from the bedroom. "Is that coffee I smell?"

Uh-oh. "You just wait there and I'll bring you some." I scrape a puddle of brew off the top of the stove into a bowl and strain as many grounds and leftover pasta as possible from it before pouring it into a coffee cup.

"What's the holdup?"

"Just getting some milk, love." I bring the mug in and present it to Linda. "You getting up soon?"

Linda gives me a beaming smile. "No, I think I'll just stay here and drink my coffee while you wash the floor."

We set out for Tongariro National Park, just south of Lake Taupo. The park is not overly large by Canadian standards—some eighty square kilometres—but it encapsulates three volcanoes, the largest of which, Mount Ruapehu, rises to almost twenty-eight hundred metres. It is the country's oldest national park, donated by a Maori chief to Queen Victoria in 1887 to preserve its natural state. The three volcanoes create their own microclimate, their great height forcing winds to drop their moisture, which results in a tropical rain climate on the west side of the park and a desert on the east.

We turn off the main road just after Lake Taupo and head for the western entrance. Although patches of trees exist in sheltered, low-lying depressions, the soil is too poor to sustain a large tropical forest and most of the land is covered in a diverse selection of flowering scrub, with the scarred sides of the volcanoes rising steeply above it. We drive several kilometres before reaching a turnoff that takes us north, up Mount Ruapehu.

The mountain supports two ski resorts, and although the season generally runs from July to October, the road remains open year-round. We climb out of the scrublands into a region of meadows, covered with silky-topped grass, until we come to the peak. The greenish-grey volcanic debris contrasts sharply with the brilliant blue sky, where tufts of white, fluffy clouds scud past us, low and fast. In the distance, another mountain range cuts a jagged silhouette, but it cannot compare in majesty to Ruapehu. We head back, chilled and energized by the mountain air.

As we exit the park and head for the main highway, we come to a lay-by bordered by a flat pasture of brown grass, which is skirted by a smallish river, the Whangaehu. In the distance, a train trestle arcs over the river's gentle current. It is an unremarkable vista, except for the fact that, as a plaque informs us, it is the scene of one of the worst disasters in New Zealand's history. On Christmas Eve, 1953, the *Night Express* left Wellington for Auckland, with 285 people aboard. A few minutes before the express was to cross the rail bridge, a natural dam of ice at the south end of Mount Ruapehu's crater lake burst, releasing thousands of tonnes of water. As the water plunged down the steep slopes, it gathered ash, rock, and boulders into a thundering mess that channelled down the Whangaehu Valley and swept away most of the rail bridge. A young postal clerk by the name of Ellis tried to warn the engineer, but it was too late, and the engine and the first five cars plunged into the abyss, killing all on board. When the train came to a halt, one carriage tilted dangerously over the edge. Ellis and another man pulled all but one of the occupants to safety before it too plunged into the icy waters below. In all, 151 people were killed, many of their bodies never recovered, swept out to sea, some one hundred kilometres away, by the torrent.

By now, it is mid-afternoon, too early to return to our base at the Lakeview Motel, and I persuade Linda to visit one of the most unique power plants in the world. Located just north of Taupo, the Wairakei Power Plant is the world's oldest continually operating geothermal plant. Situated in the valley of the Waikato River, it is a complex mishmash of gleaming steel pipes, storage tanks, and turbine sheds, all peeking out from giant clouds of steam, emanating from stacks.

According to the tour guide, the immense magma chamber that lies under Lake Taupo is so close to the surface that groundwater is almost immediately heated past the boiling point. By drilling less than three hundred metres into the ground, engineers are able to tap into vast quantities of hot water. When it reaches the surface, it flashes to steam, which stainless-steel pipes transmit from the main drill site to the turbine generators. The plant reached its maximum output of 175 megawatts (enough, I mentally calculate, to power fifty million personal vibrators) in the 1960s. Since then, production has been slowed to allow the resource to naturally recharge, and it is expected to last well into the twenty-first century or whenever Taupo blows up again, which would make it something of a moot point, wouldn't it?

The next day, after a slightly less-gushy breakfast than the day before, we head southeast toward the city of Napier. Located on the east coast of the island, the area surrounding Napier was first mapped by Captain Cook in 1769. The region was little more than an outlying rock, attached to the mainland by a long spit, but Cook reckoned the enclosed lake would make a good sheltered port and, some eighty years later, whalers plying the Antarctic region made it a base of operations. Farmers soon set up shop, growing a wide range of vegetables, fruit, and tobacco. Today, some fifty thousand people live in the town.

Napier has one claim to fame that draws people from six continents: the largest collection of original art-deco buildings in the world. The circumstance that led to this oddity was, most unusually for New Zealand, an earthquake. On the morning of Tuesday, 3 February 1931, a tremor measuring 7.9 on the Richter scale hit the town, killing a score of people and demolishing the central business district. The ensuing reconstruction occurred just at the height of the art-deco movement, and Kiwi architects, inspired by their European counterparts, went nuts, plastering the town with modern, angular buildings to the point where, frankly, the locals got right sick of it. The four dozen or so commercial and public buildings gradually fell into disrepair, and some were even knocked down, before the local citizenry realized what a unique treasure they had. Now, of course, the town is all spruced up for a Kodak moment.

We arrive mid-morning, the sun beating down on the aquamarine waters in the broad bay. The warm ocean currents on the east coast of the North Island endow the town with a moderate climate year-round; the swaying palm trees that line the streets put me in mind of a Mediterranean shore. Several fancy hotels are located on Marine Parade, the road running adjacent to the beach, but we opt for something slightly inland—the Coral Gables Inn. There isn't a reef in sight and the roof is utterly devoid of gables, but the grounds are spotless and the Pamplona-red exterior shrieks discount rates. We register with Sid, our host, and check into our ground-floor suite.

Coral Gables is an excellent choice. Not only is it comfortable and admirably cheap, but it is also within a hundred metres of the sea. We change into our running gear and go for a jog along the shore. The pebble beach is not the best footing to run on, but the view is fantastic. To the east, the ocean stretches in an endless, rippling turquoise plain, while to the south, the white cliffs of Cape Kidnappers glimmer in the noon sun. The cape is named for an incident in 1769, when a group of Maoris, no doubt tired of eating boobies, decided to have one of Captain Cook's crew for dinner instead. Although they were unsuccessful, their attempt was recorded for geographic posterity.

We come to the statue of Pania of the Reef, a life-sized bronze of a young woman wearing nothing but a grass skirt and a smile. Pania, according to Maori folklore, was a beautiful maiden who spent her days swimming with sea creatures before retiring at night to a stream delta, near the present town of Napier. One day, a handsome warrior by the name of Karitoki came to the stream for a drink and when Pania spotted him, the love bug bit her. They were secretly married and spent their nights making whoopee in his shack, but every morning before dawn she had to return to the sea or die.

Naturally, Karitoki's pals wondered why he was dragging his *tiki* around all day and didn't believe his tale about a sea maiden, even when he showed them the hickies. A witch doctor who knew all about sea maidens counselled Karitoki that if he put some cooked food in Pania's mouth while she slept, she would never be able to return to the sea. That night, Karitoki obediently dropped a coconut fritter into his girlfriend's mouth, but she awoke, spat out the food, and dashed off to the sea, never to be seen again.

Nobody is quite sure why Pania never returned. Some say she was dismayed by his treachery; others think she was concerned about her weight. But whatever the reason, during a full moon, legend says you can see a vision of her below the waves, imploring her lover with her hands. Judging from the way her statue's breasts have been polished to a bright sheen, it appears that some of the local Napier lads have been doing a little imploring of their own.

We head back to the Coral Gables for a shower, then walk into town. As advertised, the main business district is stuffed with art-deco buildings, including the *Daily Telegraph* office and

several banks, hotels, and restaurants. Most of them are physically small, but the embellishments of columns, stylized plant life,
and vertically oriented windows give them a bursting-with-pride
quality that is cheerfully endearing in a vain kind of way. I
especially enjoy the generous use of pastel colours, which make
me feel as if I'm wandering around an outdoor candy store.

We are distracted by several gardens—spacious, quiet retreats
filled with enough tropical flora to make me itch. One area is
dedicated to a score of different varieties of rose bushes, and
although I am mightily tempted to steal a few of the more magnificent samples, I limit myself to chaste sniffs. We decide instead to
take photos, an entire roll, in fact, and have to head back into
town to drop it off for developing. The camera shop sits near the
Daily Telegraph, in a small commercial mall. The proprietor is a
woman in her late thirties, with short blonde hair, who, as befits
the weather, is wearing a sleeveless top and khaki shorts.

"Where are you from?" she asks, when she hears our accents.
We say Calgary. "My brother is in Banff. He loves it there." She
introduces herself as Sue and promptly invites us to dinner the
following evening. When we attempt to protest the imposition,
she will have none of it.

On the way back to the motel, we stop at a grocery store and
pick up some salmon steaks. We then visit a bottle shop, where
the owner recommends a Chardonnay from Mission Estate,
located just a few miles inland at Taradale. "It's the best kept
secret in New Zealand," he enthuses. I suspect the worst-kept
secret is his cologne, which could double as insect repellant.

We grill dinner that night, using a mixture of mayonnaise,
Dijon mustard, and fresh dill to marinate the salmon. We splash
courgette slices with olive oil and balsamic vinegar and cook them
on the grill, along with the salmon. The meal is rounded out with
baked potatoes, sour cream, and chives. True to the wine
merchant's word, the Mission Estate Chardonnay goes very well

with the meal. Later, I ask Sid about the winery.

"Make sure you go for lunch," he says. "They have an excellent restaurant there—it's pricey, but worth the trip."

I return to our room and tell Linda about the conversation. "What do you think?" I ask.

"I think you should take me there tomorrow for my birthday. It would be the perfect place to celebrate."

The next morning, after a leisurely run, Linda and I set off around the large harbour toward Taradale. At the very end of the Second World War, the German U-boat u862 snuck into Napier's port, and the captain and his crew rowed ashore under cover of darkness and supposedly engaged in cow milking, something not normally found in the submariner's manual of mayhem. There's no mention of what they did to neighbourhood sheep, however, which we later encounter clogging up the road to Mission Estate. I honk the horn, and a black-and-white border collie comes running to herd them off the blacktop.

As we near Taradale, the apple and peach orchards give way to row after row of vines ready for picking. Shotgun blasts, presumably to scare the birds off, periodically rend the air. We reach the turnoff and follow a row of mature plane trees toward the winery. The main building is the old seminary, a two-storey, wooden building painted white, with blue trim. Two wings branching off it surround a cobbled courtyard, in which a fountain tinkles merrily in the centre.

Mission Estate was founded in 1851 by the Society of Mary, created in Lyon, France. The order dedicated itself to converting the heathen, et cetera, but that didn't stop them from planting grapes and fermenting enough sacramental wine to keep everyone in the country permanently full of the Holy Spirit. Their order proved so popular that they had to expand the premises several times to accommodate all the young men who heeded the calling, adjacent to their wine presses.

We join the morning tour, where Bernard, a friendly monk in khaki shorts, explains the background of the order. Although the wine business remains on the property, the seminary is now housed in Auckland, and the mission is used for conferences, weddings, and other celebrations.

After a tasting in the cellar, we retire to the restaurant. Lunch is served out on the patio, where a dozen tables are scattered under large canvas umbrellas. We settle into comfortable wicker chairs and admire the view, fields of bright green vines rolling gently downward toward Hawke Bay in the distance. As an appetizer, we order the pumpkin, coconut, and seafood chowder, spiced with red curry paste. For my main course, I resist the twice-braised pork belly in vanilla sauce and opt instead for the char-grilled fillet of beef, with thyme rub. Linda has grilled *mahi mahi*, smothered with vermouth cream sauce and served on a bed of lettuce. Both dishes are accompanied by the proper wines: a Sauvignon Blanc for Linda and a Cabernet Sauvignon for me. We toast her birthday. For dessert, the waiter convinces us to have the Mission Tiramisu, which is layered with mascarpone, chocolate, and Italian sponge cake soaked in brandy.

After the meal, they roll us out to the car on wine-barrel dollies, where we promptly take a nap. We wake up with a start some hours later. The sun is definitely waning and we have to get ready for our dinner with Sue that evening. We quickly drive back into town; fortunately, Napier's evening rush hour lasts about five minutes. After a quick buff and pomade, we are back on the road, following Sue's directions to her home.

Sue and her husband, Phil, live in a spacious suburb west of Napier. Their home is on a half hectare of land, with large pepper trees, a garage, and a pool scattered around it. Sue takes us on a tour of her home and is especially proud of a recent kitchen renovation. She serves a beef roast, with baked vegetables, and a fruity Merlot in the dining room. I silently vow to jog three extra kilometres at the next opportunity, then pick up my knife and fork and dig in.

After the meal, we refill our wine glasses and go outside to sit on the patio and watch the sun set over the hills west of town. "How do you like New Zealand so far?" asks Phil.

"We love it," I say. "The people are very friendly, the weather is gorgeous, and the countryside is beautiful."

"I've always wanted to go to Canada to live," says Sue.

"Why bother?" I wave my hand to encompass their home and the surrounding countryside. "You've got all of that here, without the cold."

"There is something that you've got that we don't," says Phil. "Opportunity."

"How do you mean?"

Sue tries to shush her husband, but Phil continues. "Did you see the photographs in our house? Sue did them."

I had noted some very beautiful landscapes while eating dinner. "They could hang in a museum," I say.

"And they should, but they don't." Phil glances at his wife. "That's why her brother went to Banff. He doesn't have half Sue's talent, but he's landed a spot at the art college there and he's the toast of the town." Sue tries to change the subject, but her husband continues. "We have a phrase for it in New Zealand, you know—the tall-poppy syndrome." He makes a slitting motion across his neck. "Anyone sticks their head too far above the rest of the crowd, it gets chopped off."

Phil stands and heads back into the house, hopefully to fetch more wine and not a scythe. Sue apologizes for his outburst, but I find it refreshing to hear a bit of criticism, as well as the fact that somebody is cranky. I guess I'm learning a thing or two—clearly, beautiful surroundings don't guarantee happiness.

At the end of the evening, we thank our hosts for the food, the wine, and the candidness. A little imperfection always makes a place more appealing, in my book. ∎

Chapter 10

The Headless Ghost

Despite the art deco, the rose gardens, and the Coral Gables' beautiful barbecue, the enchantment of Napier soon begins to pale. We pull out the guidebook and consider our next destination. Our plan is to head toward Wellington, some two hundred kilometres south. We aren't particularly interested in spending time in the capital, but it's where we can catch the ferry across Cook Strait to the South Island.

I call the ferry service to make a reservation, but the booking clerk informs that there has been a delay. One of the ferries hit a reef, near the South Island terminal of Picton, which gouged a large hole beneath its waterline, and the regular schedule is on hold until the stricken vessel can be replaced.

"Go and spend a few days in Wellington—it's worth it," advises Sid. "It's a tad expensive, but there's lots to see and do."

We load up the Egg and bid adieu to Napier, paying our respects to Pania as we leave town. Her shiny breasts, glistening in the sun, point in the direction of Wellington. I take this as an auspicious sign.

The sun soon gives way to low cloud, however, and it rains for most of the morning as we drive south, but when we crest the high ground that rings the city, it abruptly lets up. From the forest-covered hills that surround us, Wellington proper descends in a neat and tidy, Anglo-Saxon arc of suburban homes to a large, natural harbour some five kilometres wide. Its central business district, marked by a cluster of more than one hundred high-rise buildings, rests in a flat portion of the basin near the mouth of the harbour.

The first people to live in the area were Maori tribes, who set up camp a thousand years ago, then wisely decamped due to seismic activity. The first Europeans arrived in the 1830s and, after taking in the broad hills that surround the harbour, promptly settled in a swamp and christened their new home Wellington, after the victor of the Battle of Waterloo. (In a way, it's a relief that Napoleon didn't win; he favoured names like Wagram and Hoche.)

When the original settlement inevitably began to sink into the swamp, Wellingtonians upped sticks and resettled at the site of the current central business district, which offered dryer ground, fewer mosquitoes—and a major fault line that was revealed in 1855 when the largest earthquake ever recorded in New Zealand struck the town. The ground was pushed up by about three metres, so the industrious, if not a tad thick, residents extended their town an extra several hundred metres out into the bay on the newly minted land. Impressed by their resourcefulness, the governor general shifted the capital from Auckland to Wellington in 1865, where it has resided, somewhat shakily, ever since.

Significant earthquakes rock the city several times a year, to the point where the half million current inhabitants are rather fatalistic about it all. Most disaster planning consists of constructing homes from wood, which I suppose is considered a handy source of tinder in the event of calamity.

We arrive in Wellington in the midst of the New Zealand International Arts Festival, a biennial event that sees performers gathering from all over the world to strut their stuff. As we drive to the centre of town, the streets are filled with soggy mimes and baggy-trousered clowns negotiating puddles on stilts.

Thanks to the festival, every reasonably priced inn is crammed to the rafters with cultural riff-raff, and we are forced to rent a room at one of the most expensive hotels in town.

Our refuge is an imposing box of early-twentieth-century brick, which manages to combine the *savoir faire* of a Victorian men's club with the charm of a Transylvanian castle. We pay the ironically dubbed "Celebration Rate," which is double the normal cost; I assume that the owners take glee in extortion.

The elevator operator, a grey-skinned man, escorts us to the top floor. The hallway is decorated with suits of armour and has thick, oak floorboards, which creak as we walk to the end of the hall. Our "suite" consists of a long, narrow room, with two single beds at one end and a pair of under-stuffed chairs positioned in front of a ten-inch, black-and-white TV at the other. From our bathroom window, we have an excellent view of a massive neon sign that blinks "DRAWDE GNIK" every ten seconds or so, its red light illuminating several gargoyles that glower stonily into the gloom.

We head back to the lobby and glower in similar fashion out at the street. The rain is once again coming down in buckets. Kevin, the check-in clerk, a thin, chinless man, clears his throat. "Not a very nice day out for a stroll, is it?" I admire his grasp of the obvious; if Kevin were a coroner, I suspect his autopsies would conclude that the corpse was full of bones.

Kevin pulls a festival brochure from a pile and flips it open to the theatre page. "If you're looking for something to do, I'd recommend you go see *Henry VIII*. It's playing this afternoon."

I glance at the particulars. It's reasonably priced, but you have to be careful at these festivals, so I ask, "It's not a *fringe* play, is it?"

Kevin's eyebrows arch in offended astonishment. "Heavens, *no!*" They don't go for any of that artsy-fartsy truck around here, I'm told.

We call the box office and reserve two places, and Kevin directs us to the bus that will take us to the venue. After travelling some fifteen minutes through the downtown core, the bus enters a seedy commercial street lined with pawnshops, liquor stores, and wholesale sheep-shearing outlets. The driver calls out our stop and helpfully points us in the direction of the theatre. Linda and I walk up an alleyway lined with overflowing garbage bins, until we arrive at a sandwich board that directs us up a fire escape.

I am beginning to think that someone has gone to rather elaborate extremes to tease the crap out of us, but when we arrive at the top of the metal stairs, a woman with brilliant orange hair and a beaming smile escorts us inside. We purchase our tickets at the box office, before descending a second stairwell that reeks of greasepaint and stale bacon.

The venue is a disused meat locker, which has been converted into a stage, with the addition of a set of bleachers. Taking our seats in Row Three, Linda and I peruse the program to discover that all of the male roles are being played by women, and vice versa. The lights dim and Cardinal Wolsey makes his entrance, riding on a meathook. We are then treated to some ninety minutes of fireworks, simulated oral sex, and general mayhem. I must say both Linda and I enjoyed Henry VIII flashing his tits, but it makes me wonder what you have to do for bona fide fringe cred in this town.

Linda and I return to the hotel and, after an invigorating pepperoni pizza at a trattoria around the corner, venture forth into the evening. It is starting to rain again, so Kevin loans us a large umbrella and points us in the direction of the waterfront, where we discover the Boatshed, a long, low shack, which, once upon a time, housed scullers and their long rowboats, but has long been cleared of muscles, and now houses a clam joint and a performance venue. We arrive just in time to see a performance by the World's Biggest Little Opera Company, which sings a fine selection of arias from the works of Giuseppe Verdi. Normally, I'm not a fan of opera, but the company performed the selections with such verve, wit, and charm that I join the standing ovation at the end, even though none of them took off a stitch of clothing. Maybe there's hope for the festival yet. After the performance, we return to the hotel to be lulled to sleep by the rhythmic red flash of "DRAWDE GNIK."

The following morning, I call the ferry service to see if they've replaced their broken boat yet. "I'm sorry, sir, your crossing is going to be delayed until tomorrow," I'm told.

Oh, well, at least the rain has let up. We decide to make the best of it and see the town. The buildings that grace downtown Wellington are an eclectic mix of wooden nineteenth-century colonial, art deco, and modern, all jumbled together. No doubt, the city planning commission is fully aware that they will all be knocked down in the next earthquake. We set out along the waterfront on a pedestrian walk that takes us past the national museum and various abstract-art installations. We come to Frank Kitts Park, a large, open area with lawns and a kids' play area, which features a number of devices guaranteed to wring juvenile necks. About halfway through the park, Linda and I stop to admire a memorial that resembles the foremast of a ship. "It belongs to the *Wahine* ferry," explains a passing constable, who is patrolling the park on foot. "It was one of the worst sea disasters in New Zealand history."

Always eager for a good disaster, we pause to hear the story. According to the policeman, the *Wahine* was the overnight ferry that travelled to Wellington from Christchurch on the South Island. On the morning of 10 April 1968, it reached Wellington just as two cyclones collided in the Cook Strait. The ferry's captain tried to negotiate the narrow entrance to the harbour, but winds exceeding 250 kilometres an hour blew the ship onto the rocks of Barrett Reef. Tugs couldn't reach it because the winds were too nasty.

As TV crews filmed the ferry being battered against the rocks, the captain finally gave the order to abandon ship. Four lifeboats were lowered into the water, but two foundered in the high waves and every man, woman, and child was on their own as they hopped into the strait. Fortunately, most of the 610 passengers were plucked safely from the waters, but some 200 were pushed toward the shore.

"Over 50 were killed," says the constable. "Some were

drowned, some battered against the rocks, but most died of fright." He bows his head a moment in solemn memory, then continues the conversation on a more cheerful note. "So, where are you off to after Wellington?"

"We're taking the ferry to the South Island."

"Ah." He clears his throat once or twice. "Well, I must be off, then. Enjoy your stay."

Thus cheered, we continue our walk. A detour up a side street takes us to higher ground, where we encounter New Zealand's Parliament building. Built in the nineteenth century, it is a staid, four-storey wooden affair painted a mellow yellow. Right next door is the much livelier—indeed, bizarre—Executive Wing. Built in 1981 and immediately nicknamed the Beehive, it is a circular, ten-storey building, resembling the popular hairdo of the fifties. Rather than housing a salon, however, it serves as the offices of the prime minister and his Cabinet. It is so wonderfully hideous that I am charmed immensely. When we get back to our hotel, I mention this to Kevin, who assures me that every prime minister who has ever resided there hated it.

"The rooms are all pie-shaped. You can't get anything more than a desk and two chairs in them," he says. I imagine they also have to get L'Oreal in to recolour the exterior every few months.

That evening, we return to the Boatshed, where we watch a performance by the Kronos Quartet, a San Francisco ensemble made up of two violins, a viola, and a cello. They specialize in modern music from composers such as Philip Glass and Steve Reich, although their repertoire includes a wide range of styles and inspirations. I especially enjoy their version of Jimi Hendrix's "Purple Haze," as well as a composition by Raymond Scott entitled "Dinner Music for a Pack of Hungry Cannibals."

The latter puts us in the mood for dinner, but by the time the concert is finished, it's late and all the restaurants in the area are closed. The rain has returned, and we are reluctant to venture further afield. Heading back to the hotel, we ascend to our room, tired, soggy, and hungry. It is almost midnight when we retire. The wind is howling and the building is creaking and groaning, but I still manage to fall asleep, my empty stomach grumbling in protest.

I awake from my slumber with a start; somewhere nearby, a door has slammed shut with a loud *bang*. At first, I think it's just the wind, but when I glance toward the entrance to our room, I see the unmistakable silhouette of someone standing, motionless, near the portal. I blink once to clear my vision, but it is definitely there—a dark torso and legs pressing against the wall, the head invisible, like a ghost. Obviously, a cat burglar has snuck in, only to have the wind slam the door behind him.

My heart pounding, I try to think what to do. Is he aware that I am awake? Is he standing motionless, hoping that I won't see him in the dark? Worse still, is he armed? I glance around, but the only weapons within my grasp are a bedside lamp and my pillow. I peer back at the burglar, who is still standing perfectly motionless. I decide upon my plan of action. Screwing up my courage, I sit up and fling the pillow, shouting "Get out!" as loudly as possible.

Linda, who was sound asleep, literally leaps from her bed. "What's wrong?"

There's good news and bad news. The good news is that the intruder isn't a burglar after all. The bad news is that it appears to be a headless ghost. "Don't you see it?" I shriek.

Linda stares in panic. "What?"

"The *thing*."

"Where?"

"By the door."

At this point, Linda has the presence of mind to turn on the bedside lamp and the apparition disappears. I arise and slowly approach the door. I glance outside, but there is no one in the hall, only the eerie, low whistling of the wind. I close the door and return to the bed. Linda is staring at me as if I have cut loose for Planet Neeboo.

"Just watch," I say. I turn off the lamp and, once again, the ghostly silhouette is visible. "See?"

Linda nods. It must be a trick of the light, but why didn't we notice it the night before? It suddenly occurs to me: the large, red sign outside is no longer flashing. Most of the exterior roof lights must be turned off after midnight. Sure enough, when I close the bathroom door, it cuts off the remaining light coming through the window, eliminating the ghostly outline. I return to bed and shut off the light, but even though I have a rational explanation for the mystery, I sleep the rest of the night with one eye open, terrified.

Mind you, I forget all about feeling hungry.

The next afternoon, we make our way to Wellington Harbour's Inter-Island Wharf, where we follow a crew of pimply dockworkers waving bright orange cones, as they direct us in line for our ferry. The *Tikitaki*, about 120 metres long and 60 metres at her beam, is capable of carrying eight hundred passengers and seventy cars at twenty knots in rough seas. Were it not for the recently patched hole beneath her waterline, I'd feel quite confident.

In the interest of full disclosure, I should mention that I am not the happiest of seafarers, although my ancestors include several pirates, whose nicknames were generally along the lines of Bilious Bart and Jelly Bowels Jake. In their defence, it's also interesting to note that most buccaneers died of dysentery rather than as head guest at a necktie party.

We board the craft in orderly fashion, directed by a first mate into the hold, where the Egg is lashed down with chains and winches. We are then escorted up a flight of stairs to the passenger area, which includes several restaurants, a tuck shop, and a video arcade. I glance briefly into the arcade to see if there is anything along the lines of *The Poseidon Adventure*, but the ferry operators have forgone such appropriate themes in favour of *Grand Prix Smashups* & *Alien Bounty Hunter*. The cafeteria, I note, is featuring macaroni and cheese—good, viscous stuff that will stick to the plate in the event of turbulent seas. I find a nice interior lounge that looks as if it's securely bolted down, but unfortunately, the bar stools do not come with seatbelts. I sigh and order a bottle of beer.

The first part of the three-hour journey through the harbour and surrounding headlands is relatively tranquil. Finishing my beer, I release my grip from a bulkhead and take a few tentative steps. The gentle, rolling pitch is no problem; I seem to have found my sea legs. Linda and I swagger out to the deck and make our way to the bow, where we stand and survey Cook Strait.

First discovered by you-know-who in 1770, the strait is only twenty-three kilometres wide at its narrowest point. To the southwest, in the setting sun, I can make out the distant silhouette of Marlborough Sounds, the fingers of rock that mark the South Island's most northerly tip.

An elderly man, his face leathered by years in the sun, is leaning against the rail, also admiring the sunset.

"Not a bad day for a crossing," I say.

He turns slightly and looks at me with one deep-blue eye. "It's never a good day for a crossing, lad. One moment it can be clear as glass, and the next thing you know, the Roaring Forties blow in."

"What are they?"

"The fiercest winds a sailor can ever encounter. They say the devil *hisself* doesn't dare venture forth when they're up."

I thank him for this edifying information and, taking Linda by the elbow, calmly return indoors. Just as we reach the lounge, the *Tikitaki* hits the open seas and her hull begins to pitch up and down in earnest. Fortunately, the ship's pharmacy carries a full range of nausea-suppression aids, including Gravol, Chi pressure-point bracelets, and medals of St. Anthony. Linda purchases a magazine and returns to the lounge, while I larder up and go in search of a mast to lash myself to. After an hour or so, we enter Queen Charlotte Sound, which leads to Picton. The sound is a long, sinuous channel formed by an ancient glacier, and the surrounding land immediately becalms the water. I am relieved enough to go on the deck once more.

By now, it is dark, but the wooded hills are lit by a full moon. We glide beneath a mantle of stars, the inky black waters foaming in the phosphorescent wake. As we near the point where the ferry was hulled by a reef just a few days earlier, I try to suppress any thoughts of the captain, completely legless from drinking a quart of rum, softly humming "Yo-ho-ho," as he hangs draped over the helm.

We pass the mishap scene without incident, however, and by midnight, Picton comes into view, its wharf glimmering with lights and civilization. Up the hill, I can see the blinking neon sign of the motel where we will stay the night. The crew manages to dock the boat without inflicting further punctures, and we return to the hold for the vehicle-unchaining ceremony, before disembarking down a ramp onto terra firma. Once we are safely ashore, I pull over to the edge of the wharf and toss my medals and other superstitious paraphernalia into the sea. It is only as we drive off that it occurs to me: we eventually have to go back.

Picton, says a local brochure, is the ideal spot for holidaying—one can participate in a wide assortment of swimming, diving, camping, and frolicking. Personally, I recommend leaving. We arise and, after a quick coffee in a local shop, head to the south end of Picton, where the road branches in two directions: east toward Blenheim and west toward Nelson.

Blenheim, located at the mouth of the Wairau River, is named for the battle that took place in 1704 near a village of the same name in Bavaria. It was a major victory for the English, under the Duke of Marlborough, and her allies against Louis XIV. After the battle, King Louis decided he would rather build Versailles than conquer Europe, thus giving generations of tourists somewhere to go. Marlborough returned to England and built Blenheim Palace, the eventual birthplace of Winston Churchill.

Westward is Nelson, named after Viscount Horatio Nelson, victor at the Battle of Trafalgar in 1805. Mind you, Nelson happened to catch a bullet during the festivities and died, but he was pickled in brandy and shipped back to London for a state funeral, which is reason enough for me to choose to head west.

We motor leisurely along a two-lane road that winds its way around the Marlborough Sounds. I must say, now that I can observe it in full daylight, I am much less impressed. The forests covering the hills have a scruffy, unkempt look about them—a good fire or two would spruce things up. I explain this to Linda, who concludes I am badly in need of lunch.

We pull over at an antique shop and deli in the town of Havelock, where we feast on some Black Forest ham sandwiches, beside a mouldy collection of butter churners and oxen harnesses. For some reason that I cannot begin to fathom, the proprietor has collected an impressive display of dark, scrappy lumps of woolly detritus, which appear to be something the cook pulls out of his sink trap at periodic intervals. I compliment Linda on her choice of eatery.

We traverse the Wai Whangamoa forest, and the highway drops toward the coast. Before us spreads Tasman Bay, which holds the distinction of apparently being the only geographic region in New Zealand not named by, or after, Captain Cook. Tasman Bay got its name from Abel Tasman, a Dutch explorer who visited the South Seas in the 1640s. When he anchored at Separation Point across the bay and attempted to greet the locals, a Maori canoe promptly rammed his landing craft, killing four of his crew members. Tasman hastily retreated, marking the body of water as Murderer's Bay on his charts. The local tourist board, for reasons still unclear, later decided to change the name.

We arrive in Nelson by early afternoon. Although it is early

March and thus the beginning of fall, the town, nestled in the long bay, is sheltered by mountain ranges to the west from the worst weather that can plague the South Island. Nelson is one of the sunniest places in New Zealand, and this is reflected in the tanned, open countenances of its citizens. On the other hand, Nelson is also a centre of wine cultivation, and they could all be as cheerfully pissed as newts, for all I know.

We pull into the New Grennville Hotel, located on Rocks Road, which runs along the beach that skirts the western part of town. It is surprisingly modern and appears to be constructed from wood and drywall, as opposed to the traditional cinder block and tin that we have been enjoying for so long.

Lorrie, the hotelier, takes us on a tour of her domain. She has decorated the motel in dusty rose and forest green, a soothing combination that makes us feel instantly at home. The kitchen is equipped with a drip-style coffee percolator, for which Linda is grateful, as well as a complete video selection of Richard Gere's movies, for which I am ecstatic. We immediately check in, change into our shorts and running shoes, and go for a jog along the beach.

As we are running, we come upon a group of Maori boys, fishing on the shore. Most traditional shore fishermen, like Malcolm back in Manly, use long, fibreglass poles, which allow them to cast a lure and bait out over the surf into less-agitated waters, where fish are more likely to lurk. These boys have adopted a different technique, however. They have constructed a large kite and, using the offshore breeze, have positioned it some thirty metres out to sea and fifteen metres up. A long, baited line, acting as a tail, dangles from the kite into the water. While one boy tends to the kite, a second boy minds a line that runs through the surf out to the hook; in the case of a bite, he can pull in his catch without grounding the kite. The third boy pulls a basket out of the surf to show off his catch: half a dozen white fish. I am about to compliment them on their ingenuity when the line jerks—something has taken the bait, and they squeal in delight. I am suddenly reminded of the joy that the young boy in Raro experienced while collecting crabs in the tidal pools. We stand and encourage them as they pull it in, laughing at their infectious, childish happiness.

We reach the Tahunanui Beach Reserve, which is a pleasant park covered with tall palms and grass. *Tahunanui* is the Maori word for the Southern Lights, the antipodean version of the aurora borealis. Considering that the Maori are a martial people, and one of the few Aboriginal cultures never to be conquered by Europeans, I can't help but notice that many of their place names are quite poetic. *Whangarei*, for instance, is the term for "bountiful land." European names, on the other hand, tend to reflect warriors or battles. Of course, Beeby's Knob, an otherwise undistinguished hill some thirty kilometres south of Nelson, isn't exactly blood-curdling, but you get the drift.

Having exhausted our lungs and legs, we return to the New Grennville and shower off, before heading into town to buy food for dinner. One of the great treats of New Zealand cuisine are mussels, huge, fleshy things plucked from nearby beaches and sold by the metric tonne. We buy a large ladleful and return to the motel, where we fry up some onion and garlic and add chopped tomatoes, white wine, and fresh basil to create the Marseilles version of *moules*. We sop up the stew with a French baguette and then retire for the evening.

The next morning, like just about every morning in Nelson, dawns bright and clear. After breakfast and a brief walk along the beach, we hop into the Egg and head west for wine country. Although Blenheim is considered the wine capital of the South Island, as it produces the bulk of export wines, the area west of Nelson has a number of smaller wineries, noted for their fine liquid produce.

Our first stop is Appleby, just south of Rabbit Island, a flat stretch of land known, not surprisingly, for its apple orchards.

In the midst of all the Granny Smiths, however, are several hectares of vines. A sign beckons us to turn off the road toward one of the vineyards. Taking our cue, we turn at the next right.

Seifried Estates is housed in what appears to be a cross between a Swiss chalet and a Bohemian castle, a charming jumble of architectural oddities perched in the middle of a field of vines. The family originates in Austria and specializes in white wines, so we decide to sample their Chardonnay, which is thick and fruity, with an aftertaste of butterscotch that lingers till Easter. Although it is well out of our budget, we decide on the spot to buy a dozen bottles of it; most of Nelson's boutique wines are consumed in-country and there's no telling when we'll see it again. We thank the vintners and continue on our way, chuffed by our discovery and eager to continue exploring further.

The plain around Appleby soon gives way to higher country, and we climb a series of rolling hills to the town of Upper Moutere. The town used to be called Sarau, in honour of the German immigrants who pioneered the area, but the name was changed when U-boats started abusing the bovine population. The higher altitude and cooler nights are more suitable to the Sauvignon Blanc vine, and we search for a winery that specializes in New Zealand's signature grape.

Kahurangi Estate sits just outside Upper Moutere, near the village of Neudorf. Its three-storey turret rises proudly above the surrounding olive trees and palms. The estate features an outdoor café, where you can sit and sip their wines over a lunch platter of cheese, breads, salad, and dressings made from their own olive oil.

We are sitting on the patio beneath the shade of an olive tree, enjoying our platter, when a small, friendly bird perched on a limb above splats a load of used bugs on our table. A young waiter appears and shoos the bird away, then holds up a hand when I attempt to wipe up the mess with a paper napkin. "No worries— I'll get it." He pulls a small, plastic shoehorn out of his pants pocket and neatly picks up the offending matter.

I must admit, I'm impressed. Women have the general advantage of a purse to accommodate everything they might need in the course of a day, from spare hosiery to a small axe, but men have to be relatively selective about their accessories. Those of delicate constitutions, like my pal John, for instance, tend to carry monogrammed handkerchiefs, in case they need to sneeze, while more rugged individuals attach combination tool kits to their belts, so they can repair a combine or perform an appendectomy on an elk when and if called upon. Most of us compromise to some extent, relying on our shirt sleeves for the former and a Swiss army knife for the latter, then adding various paraphernalia as conditions warrant. I've never, however, put a shoehorn in my back pocket on the chance I'll have to shovel bird crap from the dinner table.

I am feeling quite relaxed as we drive back to Nelson, which almost proves our undoing. As we round a wide corner halfway up a steep hill, I glance out to admire the vista below—a vast carpet of green orchards sweeping along the Waimea River Valley until it encounters the deep blue waters of Tasman Bay. I return my gaze to the road just in time to see two cars coming directly at us. Two lunatics are drag racing around a blind corner and one of them has occupied our lane.

I swerve frantically onto the side of the road, inches from the precipice, as they roar past. I stop the car, get out, and curse them roundly for several minutes until I stop shaking.

We return to our hotel in Nelson, but it takes about three bottles of Seifried Chardonnay to get my heart rate down below two hundred. Thank heaven, the New Grennville's film library includes *King David*. I insert it into the VCR and settle down on the floor to watch Richard Gere mooning over Bathsheba, as she rubs herself in baby oil. Within three minutes, I am fast asleep, face down on the rug.

Thank you, Richard. ▪

CHAPTER 11

Queenstown Beckons

There's something about being almost killed by morons that tends to take the charm off a place. The next morning, we pack our bags, bid adieu to Lorrie, and continue south along Highway 6 to the west coast.

Cut off from the rest of the South Island, except for a few roads that traverse the South Alps, the west coast stretches for several hundred kilometres through some of the most beautiful—and isolated—scenery on Earth. Massive glacier tongues work their way down from snow-capped peaks into thick, tropical forests. The surf pounds upon countless craggy shores, carving intricate bays and capes. The Tasman Sea, a deep blue sparkling expanse of foamy caps, stretches in unimpeded majesty for two thousand kilometres to the Australian coast.

We reach Westport, the northernmost town of any consequence. It is situated on the lee side of Cape Foulwind, so named by Captain Cook in 1770 after eating a particularly nasty curry. The town itself served as a port for coal and gold mining operations in the 1800s and still has quite a frontier atmosphere about it, if you happen to use surly, hirsute inhabitants and greasy-spoon restaurants to define the term. We venture into a takeout joint that has squid pizza as the day's special and order one from a woman with sideburns that Elvis would envy.

The nicest part of Westport is the lovely shore view to the north, which consists of a fine sandy beach, stretching for so many kilometres into the distance that its end point is lost in the glowing mist. Even though it is within easy walking distance of town, it is entirely deserted. I am reminded of Jane Campion's film *The Piano*, in which the heroine, in an arranged marriage, arrives by boat in a pioneer New Zealand settlement, whereupon her new husband abandons her piano on a beach just like the one below us. I don't spot any soggy musical instruments, but I do have Michael Nyman's score for the movie on tape. As we sit on a bluff eating marine pizza, his tunes swirl out across the bay, keeping time with the rhythmic pounding of surf along the shore. Linda and I finish our lunch, chucking the remains of crust to the appreciative seabirds that circle above.

Just south of Westport are the Pancake Rocks, an outcrop of bedded brown limestone that the sea has carved into a series of pinnacles that look remarkably like, you guessed it, sausage and eggs. The local authorities built a gravel parking lot large enough to hold at least thirty buses, no doubt under the delusion that they were about to experience an inundation of Japanese tourists and other noted flapjack fanciers. Even for a rock lover like myself, it's not the most compelling sight, but it's a lovely day, so we decide to pull over and have a gander. Although you can scramble over the rocks unimpeded by pancake wardens, we heed a warning sign to stay off. The shore has been undermined by the surf, creating caverns and blowholes from which spray periodically spews, and I have a vision of falling through a fissure and being pounded into seagull chow. So warned, we limit our interaction with Pancake Rocks to taking a few photos.

We return to the car to be greeted by one of the homeliest birds I have ever seen. It stands about thirty centimetres tall and its dark grey, feathery body is almost completely round, except for a tiny, white head sticking out like a pimple on top. It has appeared from beneath some scraggly bushes bordering the car park and peeps plaintively until we give it a cracker. It then disappears back into the shrubs, where we hear it noisily consuming its prize. I must say, for such an ugly little fellow, he seems completely gleeful in his good fortune. I can't decide if this is some innate, mammalian manifestation of the mysterious nature of happiness or the origin of the term "birdbrain." Sometimes, it's best not to over think these things.

We enter Westland National Park, where the glacier-capped South Alps intersect the coast. Our first stop is the Franz Josef Glacier, located a few kilometres east of the highway. Thousands of years ago, the glacier lobe extended to the sea, some ten kilometres to the west, but snowfall within the immense ice caps high in the Alps has been insufficient to replenish the load, and the terminus of the glacier has retreated almost twenty kilometres inland.

A side road, starting in dense palm forest, follows the U-shaped valley upward, until you come to the terminus, a huge mash of rock ranging from boulders the size of a house down to finely ground powder. The glacier itself is minty blue in the centre, fading to a dirty grey at its sides. Water from the base of the glacier gushes through the moraine rock to form the headwaters of the Waiho River, and the river then pours, untamed and unmolested, into the Tasman Sea. It is an overcast day, and the cool air rushing down the valley is a marked contrast to the warm breezes on the coast.

As we drive farther south, the villages become tinier and more isolated. Even the road begins to narrow, as if the lack of traffic is making it shrink. At several points, bridges across gorges turn into one-lane affairs, on which a pair of rails runs down the centre, and signs at each end warn travellers to check for oncoming locomotives before proceeding. You wouldn't want to take a wrong turn and wander too far afield, but fortunately, I have a set of detailed maps, courtesy of the New Zealand Automobile Association. It takes six maps to cover the entire South Island, the scale about ten kilometres to the inch, small enough to show the panoply of streams, forests, mountain ranges, and villages sprinkled across the countryside. The detail is sufficiently fine that you can distinguish each jog in the tiniest of roads, which is handy if one has to show one's spouse that one is indeed not lost. In all modesty, I must say that this situation rarely personally arises, as my years working in the Canadian bush as a prospector sharpened my ability to the point where I rarely misplace myself geographically while sober.

Until now, of course. Highway 6 swings inland from the coast, taking us past several pristine lakes amid forest-covered hills. Linda has dozed off, and I motor along at a modest clip, trying to dampen the swaying of the car as we pass through a series of tight curves so as not to wake her up. To the left, I spot a waterfall, a cloud of mist churning through the dense foliage surrounding it, and the aqueous sight irresistibly inspires my bladder.

I pull into a rest stop, get out of the car, and wander off behind a tree. The road and surroundings are deserted—all that disturbs the quiet of the day is the call of a bird far off in the forest. I get back into the car and return to the highway, careful not to disturb Linda's sleep. I drive for another fifteen minutes or so, and she reawakens as we enter the outskirts of a small town.

Linda blinks the sleep from her eyes, then stares out the window, confused. "Didn't we drive through here already?"

"You must have been dreaming."

"No." She points to a small café, called the Pit Stop. "There's the place we ate lunch."

I squint in amazement. She's right; we stopped here not an hour ago. I pull over to the side of the road, dig out the map, and stare at it. There's no way we could have gone in a circle on the highway, so how did I get so completely turned around? I get out of the car, map in hand, and stare at my surroundings, and then, it finally occurs to me—the sun is in the wrong place. Fall is approaching, and in the Northern Hemisphere, the sun gradually lowers toward the southern horizon; here, it does the opposite, gradually lowering toward the north. I explain this to Linda.

"I've been unconsciously orienting myself ass-backwards," I conclude.

"You've been doing that as long as I've known you, Sweetie."

Linda takes over the driving, and about an hour later, we safely reach the village of Haast, where the highway turns inland. After gassing up the car, I once again take the wheel, and we head up a large valley that bisects the South Alps. Whoever Haast was, he was quite infatuated with the sound of his name—we follow Highway 6 along the Haast River toward Haast Pass. As we climb, we leave behind the clear skies over the coast and enter dense cloud. Thanks to the range of mountains pushing moist Pacific air skyward, this region of the South Islands gets about six hundred centimetres of rain a year, and we soon find ourselves in a heavy deluge. The wipers on full, I lean forward to peer through the windscreen, trying to keep to the centre of the road and away from the sheer drop that lies unseen just to the left of us.

After several tense kilometres, Linda and I crest Haast Pass and enter into the lee of the Alps. The rain stops and the sky clears once again, as we descend the mountains and enter the plains surrounding Lake Wanaka. The lake, approximately thirty-five kilometres long, is the remnant of a deep glacial valley. We are stopped about halfway along its shore by a work crew that is digging up the road ahead. I get out of the car and pore over my trusty map. According to a blurb on the back, a great Maori chief dug Wanaka's lake bed with a huge stick. If he was moving as fast as the road crew ahead, it must have taken him one hell of a long time. I put down the map and glance toward the head of the line.

Another motorist, a man in khaki shorts and canvas hat, is standing just ahead of me, facing the crew. "Come on, rattle your *dags*!" he shouts. I laugh out loud—a *dag* is a shit-encrusted piece of wool that sticks to a sheep's rear. The man comes over and introduces himself as Nigel, a retired rancher living in the town of Wanaka, at the end of the lake. He pronounces the name with the stress on the first syllable: WANA-*ka*, instead of what I had assumed to be *Wa*-NAKA. I am silently grateful as that is our destination for the night, and it's never good form to piss off the locals by mispronouncing the name of their hometown.

I explain that Linda and I are from Canada and we are on a year-long tour of the South Pacific. As we chat, I glance casually down at the lake and spot the silhouette of a large fish, some two metres long, passing along the shore. Without a doubt, it's the largest freshwater fish I've ever seen, and if I didn't know better, I'd say it was a sturgeon.

"*Thet's* a brown trout, mate," says Nigel. "They can get to fifty pounds in this lake." I whistle in appreciation; you've got to eat a lot of bugs to get that big.

The road crew eventually finishes their nap, and we continue our journey. Nigel's admonishment to the crew brings to mind many of the genial phrases that Kiwis use in everyday conversation. Much of it is similar to Canadian slang, such as "stubby" for a short beer bottle and "rust bucket" for an old Ford, but you occasionally hear a few unique gems, such as "sparrow fart," the local term for one's first flatulence on awakening at sunrise, and "dunny," which means toilet. When someone decides to drop their pants and moon the crowd, it's called "flashing the brown eye," and when someone is crazy, they're called "mad as a meat axe."

We arrive in Wanaka near evening. Originally a sheep station, it has evolved into a thriving tourist town that caters to fishermen and boating enthusiasts in summer and skiers in winter. We find a motel near the lake and then go for a walk along the shore in search of someplace to eat. To the west, the sun is setting over the Southern Alps and the sky has taken on a cobalt hue. Wisps of cloud flutter off the peaks like brilliant crimson banners, and as we walk along, they slowly fade to burnt orange, then bright lavender, and finally grey. The scent of distant forest wafts up the lake valley and settles upon the town like dew.

A group of teenagers on skateboards directs us to a restaurant that serves excellent roast chuck, and afterward, we return to our room and sleep soundly. It was a busy and fascinating day, and tomorrow we reach Queenstown.

Everywhere we go in New Zealand, Kiwis always make one suggestion: you *have* to visit Queenstown. We are warned that the destination is a combination of Sodom and Gomorrah, granola, and Xtreme jock, all rolled into one. I've looked forward to visiting the joint for weeks.

From Wanaka, Queenstown is a leisurely fifty-kilometre drive through rolling pastureland. The going is slow, however—we have to stop for several sheep crossings—and we don't arrive until mid-morning. The town sits in the centre of the South Island, on a spit of land that juts out from the northern shores of Lake Wakatipu, a Z-shaped body of water about seventy kilometres long and five kilometres wide. The Remarkables, an aptly named, sawtoothed range of snow-capped peaks, rises east of town.

Queenstown isn't big—perhaps ten thousand souls—but it punches well above its weight class due to a sophisticated tourist pull that draws holidayers seeking year-round forms of reckless behaviour. Modestly promoting itself as "New Zealand's Premier Visitor Destination," you can jet-boat, ski, hurl yourself down cliffs in a mountain bike, mud-wrestle alligators, and tie big rubber bands to your feet and fling yourself into various convenient abysses.

As we approach the town's central business district, a brightly coloured paraglider floats across the road and lands in the large parking lot of the Gondola Motor Inn. Since this is apparently a good place to "drop in," we check into the motel. Our room is on the topmost floor, and a gable on the north side leads out to a tiny balcony. I am thrilled to note that we have a first-rate view of the nearby ski slope whence paragliders originate. With any luck, we may see one snag himself on a power line.

Queenstown has that cheery, alpine vibe that seems to infuse mountain villages around the world. I am struck by the ubiquity of shops selling quartz crystals, pyramid prisms, tie-dyed do-rags, and karmic beads; the street literally reeks of patchouli. I guess I should have expected this—Wakatipu is the Maori phrase for "lake where the demon lies." It comes from the legend of a giant who kidnaps a young woman from a nearby tribe and takes her back to the mountains. While he is asleep, her lover sneaks up to his lair and sets him on fire. His body burns the lake bed into the ground, which gradually fills up with rain. Beneath the water, however, the giant's heart still beats, causing the lake to rise and fall mysteriously. When you've got that kind of mojo going, pyramid prisms are considered a good insurance policy.

Residents also seriously like their bean. In addition to more than 140 restaurants, the town proper boasts around 30 cafés. Not bad for a place about one-hundredth the size of Paris. On our walk through town, we stop at a restaurant that is decorated in vaguely Lower-Nile style, with plinths, scarabs, and lots of wicker, a sort of "King Tut Light." The menu features wheat-grass shakes and barley-sprout sandwiches.

Our waitress, Sabrina, is sitting cross-legged in front of a slice of orange and a stick of incense, chanting a mantra. She returns to the planet long enough to bring us a pot of herbal mint tea and explain the town's vibe. "It's like, one of six points in the global force field? It's *so* together." *Fer sure*. We thank her for the geography lesson and order the vegetarian spaghetti. There's nothing like tofu balls to focus the cosmic aura.

After lunch, we continue our walk to Queenstown Gardens, a large, open space on a peninsula adjacent to the main pier. In addition to the usual roses, begonias, and such, the garden features an arboretum, with more than one hundred exotic trees. Without a doubt, my favourite is the monkey tail tree. Standing about thirty metres tall, it is an impressively ugly evergreen, with long tendrils of spiky leaves that hang all the way to the ground. The species is some sixty million years old and grows wild in the Chilean Andes, where the natives eat its seeds for a bit of monkey buzz. The gardens are so peaceful, so, like, *together*, that I begin to get a buzz of my own. Maybe there is something to this cosmic-aura business, after all.

"Do you mind if I try meditating?" I ask Linda.

"Not at all." From her knapsack, Linda pulls out a tourist brochure she has picked up from the restaurant and heads to a nearby bench. "You go right ahead. I'm going to see what's happening this week."

I find a sunny clearing between several trees and begin a Tai Chi routine, a rhythmic series of movements designed to focus the energy of the mind and body. It's been several years, mind you, but I still recall a few moves, such as tickling the tiger and gilding the lily. Slowly advancing through the routine, I rotate through a series of turns, first, facing the Remarkables, then, Lake Wakatipu, and finally the monkey tail tree. As I get into the routine, my vision enters a heightened level of sensitivity, the arboretum begins to glow a deep emerald hue, and I find myself becoming one with the greenery.

"How's it going?" calls out Linda.

"I am a tree."

"That might explain the dog peeing on you," replies Linda.

I glance down in surprise. Sure enough, a Cairn terrier has snuck up behind me to wee on my left boot. I shoo it away, but the damage is done—it's a bit difficult to tune into the galactic vibe with a wet sock. I decide that I've had enough meditation, and we head back to the inn for a bath.

Over the next several days, we settle into an entertaining routine of watching other tourists jump off bridges, roar up rivers in jet boats, and hurl down rapids in rubber boats. Mostly out of sanity, we limit our activities to relatively sedate jogging through the gardens and down the walkway that follows Lake Wakatipu.

There's another good reason for backing off the gratuitous entertainment: money. I am sitting on our tiny balcony sipping a glass of wine one evening, when Linda comes out carrying a pile of receipts. "We're getting low on dough," she announces.

"Is it bad?"

"It could be worse. We're going to have to go home sooner than later."

I shudder. "The thought of going back to work gives me the willies."

"Me, too." Linda puts her arms around me. "I don't need a big house or a fancy car. I'd rather we work for ourselves. Promise me we'll try to make it on our own when we get back?"

"I promise."

We decide upon one luxury outing in Queenstown, however—a scenic flight to Milford Sound, a drowned glacial valley located on the west coast. Although it's only forty kilometres from Queenstown as the emu flies, for years, it was virtually inaccessible by land, except by a hike over two mountain ranges. Today, there is a road into the region, a 250-kilometre, twisting trail that you'd have to be mad as a meat axe to drive. Having dined on tofu and absorbed the cosmic vibe, which has a rather calming effect, we are more inclined to cough up the coin and take a nice, safe trip by plane.

We arrange for a flight from Queenstown Airport with one of the tour operators based there. Our plane, a four-seat Cessna, looks quite modern and airworthy. Tyler the pilot, however, is about twelve years old and greets us with the happy-go-lucky grin of someone who just got his braces off. We reluctantly hop in and, after Tyler has a quick yak with the control tower, are soon airborne.

Following the shore of Lake Wakatipu, we head in a general northwest direction, crossing over Pig Island, then taking a left turn up the Caples River Valley. The steep, U-shaped valley, carved by glacial action ten thousand years ago, is draped with a cover of evergreen trees that not even the most rapacious logger could reach. As we head west, I notice that the sky is becoming overcast with thick, white clouds, a result of the same alpine phenomenon that causes the slopes west of Haast Pass to receive so much rain.

With growing trepidation, I watch as the valley floor creeps higher and higher, with no sign of a break over the curtained wall ahead. I glance at Tyler, who is happily whistling the theme song from some Saturday morning cartoon show, seemingly unaware of the calamity unfolding. Fortunately, I have flown hundreds of hours with bush pilots in northern Canada, and I know how to communicate effectively with the subspecies. I point out the windshield and emit a piercing shriek, then frantically attempt to pull off my safety harness and duck under the dashboard. Tyler immediately throws the plane into a sharp curve that brings us close enough to the sidewall of the valley to endow the plastic cover of my seat with a permanent pucker.

As we pull out of the dive and regain altitude, Tyler grins widely at the fun. "No worries—there's another pass that's usually clear." Linda's face is ghostly white, and I ponder pushing him out of the plane then and there, but decide it might be more prudent to kill him *after* we land. Tyler does indeed manage to find a clear pass, and we reach Milford Sound about fifteen minutes later. Landing on a runway cut into the shoreline, we exit the craft and take in our surroundings.

To our east is Mitre Peak, rising some 1,800 metres straight out of the Tasman Sea. Across from us are Bowen and Stirling Falls, great arcs of water tumbling some 150 metres into the fjord below. The scenery truly is gorgeous, but, without a doubt, the one aspect of Milford Sound with the most impact is the five billion or so sandflies that immediately descend upon us. Every single photo I take is blurred by the necessity to furiously wave one arm in a vain attempt to avoid the total collapse of my capillary system. Linda is in even worse shape; her arms are almost black from the creatures. "Let's get out of here!" she shouts. To hell with the expense—we hastily re-board the plane before a transfusion becomes necessary. Only when we are airborne do I realize that the sandflies have chased all thoughts of infanticide from my consciousness.

On our return journey, the clouds part and the skies take on a sapphire blue hue. We pass over turquoise alpine lakes and glaciers glistening in the sun. The mountains give way to broad, rolling hills of green pastureland, upon which countless sheep gambol. In fact, it is sufficiently calming that I decide to forgive Tyler and let him live long enough to get his own skateboard. I'm just nice that way.

We soak up Queenstown's sunny aura for several more days until, one morning, we awake to grey clouds gathering on the horizon. The weather report on the radio informs us that a storm is moving in from the south, bringing colder temperatures and precipitation. It sounds like winter is headed this way.

We walk into town to have breakfast and ponder whether we should move on. Sabrina serves us two cups of cholesterol-free coffee and stops to listen as we discuss the situation.

"Cold weather? That's so, like cool," she exclaims.

"What's cool about crappy weather?" I ask.

Sabrina points out the window at the nearby ski slope. "*Duh*, it's gonna, like, snow, you know?"

Duh, right. I go back to the inn and have a look at the Egg's tires; they'd be about as useful as a grass skirt in a snowstorm. It's time to move on, so we load up the car and check out of the motel. I must say, I'm a little sad to leave Queenstown. Even though it's been less than a week, I've warmed to the flaky quality of the local scene. I wasn't tempted to do something extreme, like throw myself off a bridge or buy a pyramid, but there's something charmingly sweet about crossing New Age mysticism with snowboards. Who knows? Maybe if we'd stuck around long enough, we might have put down roots and given workshops on living in an igloo. I might even have borrowed a fire hose and gotten revenge on that Cairn terrier.

We drive east past the Remarkables and are soon descending into the pastureland that defines the east coast. The reason the South Island's east coast is far less mountainous than its west coast is hidden miles beneath the surface, where there exists an immense, active fault that will someday tear the island in half. Two great tectonic plates, the Pacific Plate to the east and the Indian/Australian to the west, collide directly under the island. They are grinding and gnashing together at this very moment, causing the Southern Alps to grow some fifteen millimetres every year. Erosion of these growing mountains has resulted in huge alluvial fans of debris that coalesce on the eastern shore to form rich, fertile plains ideally suited to pastureland—and, as we soon discover, flooding, as well.

When the storm hits, great gobs of rain fill the mountain streams and thunder downhill toward the coast. As we drive through the deluge, reports of washed-out roads soon filter in over the radio. Although our plan is to head to Dunedin, near the southeast corner of the island, we learn that the bridge on the main highway has been washed out, so turn our attention farther north. As far as we can tell, Christchurch, the largest city on the island, is still accessible, and we turn the Egg in that direction. Linda and I arrive by late afternoon, soggy but intact.

Christchurch, named after Christchurch College at Oxford University, in England, was founded in the mid-nineteenth century by Anglican settlers. The rolling hills, fertile plains, and dormant volcanoes reminded the new inhabitants of their native land, and names such as New Brighton and Belfast abound in the suburbs. The city itself is bisected by the Avon River, a rather humble body of water, even when fed by a torrential downpour.

We arrive in the city centre, near Hagley Park, which looks ideal for running. We scout about and spot the Dorset Inn on the busy avenue that skirts the park. The innkeeper, a small man with stooped shoulders and a general air of henpeck about him, greets us with the nozzle of a Hoover vacuum when we inquire at the front desk. His name is Les, but he pronounces it in a drawl that extends to about eight syllables, before eventually trailing off.

Les doesn't have any rooms available at the inn proper, but he does have an unoccupied efficiency apartment in the annex. The annex turns out to be a small residential block, built in the 1970s, in which each apartment comes complete with avocado appliances, shag rugs, and a cat named Ginger. We immediately agree to rent.

The rain has stopped by the time we unpack our groceries and feed Ginger some leftover bagels and cream cheese. Our first thought is to go for a run in Hagley Park, but Les warns us that today someone is going to attempt the world's highest bungee jump from a helicopter there, so we demur. Instead, Linda and I head downtown, where the chances of not being dinged by a daredevil are far better. The downtown core is dominated by Christ Church, a Gothic mishmash of bell towers and rose windows. Its most charming aspect is Cathedral Square, a large pedestrian park that sits in front of it.

The square is the stomping grounds of Christchurch's most eccentric inhabitant, the Wizard of New Zealand. Dressed in a long, flowing black cape and a tall, conical hat, he is normally found atop a stepladder, holding court on a number of subjects. Today's blather seems to be something about census forms. A woman sitting on a nearby bench explains that it is a pet peeve of his; he claims to be the only Kiwi ever arrested for not filling one out. He has also been threatened with sanctions by various politicians for causing lice infestations in their constituencies. The world needs more wizards.

A less-voluble inhabitant of downtown Christchurch is the statue of Robert Scott, the British Navy captain who was the second explorer to reach the South Pole, one month after Norwegian Roald Amundsen. Tragically, Scott and his team froze to death less than eighteen kilometres from safety, when they were caught in a blizzard. His statue, carved in marble by his wife, Kathleen, shows him striding across the ice in clothing that looks a tad breezy for fifty-below.

The rain returns once again, and we are more or less confined to our apartment. A man can take only so much shag rug, however, and after a few days of Kiwi TV, I suggest we take in some local culture. The *Christchurch Star* has a review of a local theatre troupe's production of a play billed as a British sex farce. Normally, the inclusion of these three words in one phrase is enough to make every nerve cell in my body recoil, but the incessant pounding of rain has softened my cranium to the point it no longer responds to even the most dire input. Besides, having endured the Kiwi Festival version of *Henry VIII*, how bad could it possibly be? We hop into the Egg and venture forth.

The theatre, which is located in a community hall, has a proscenium that juts out into a ring of bleachers. The stage is set as an English country drawing-room, with old leather chairs and a sideboard covered with whisky bottles. The audience shuffles in and the play begins. Or rather, the *torture* begins.

From what I can gather, the plot involves a mistress dropping in for a weekend visit, not realizing that her sugar daddy is the father of her new boyfriend. It turns out that the wife is having a fling with the French cook, who decides to poison the husband with an arsenic soufflé. Everyone in the audience loves it, howling in delight with each mawkish turn of events. The cast picks up on the manic energy and starts to direct their lines back to the audience, in the Benny Hill *wink-wink, nudge-nudge* school of acting. All that's missing is a couple of busty nurses in push-up bras to complete the effect.

I begin to long for a bungee daredevil to crash through the roof and put me out of my misery, when I am saved by the intermission. Two heaping glasses of Sauvignon Blanc can't wipe out the memory of the first act, however, and when the five-minute bell rings for the next act, Linda and I take it as a starting signal and sprint from the building.

The following day, the rain lets up slightly but the roads south are still impassable. We decide, instead, on a short excursion to the Banks Peninsula. Named after Captain Cook's botanist, the peninsula is a knobby protrusion some forty kilometres long, due east of Christchurch. A whaling captain named Langlois decided to bring French colonists to the region, but by the time they arrived in 1840, the British had claimed the region. Fortunately, everyone was rather magnanimous, and the British allowed the French to set up a colony, as long as they didn't consume too many of the local amphibians. The colonists grudgingly swore allegiance to the new owners and peacefully settled down to create their own distinct settlement.

In contrast, the peninsula itself has a far more violent history, having been created when two adjacent volcanoes emerged from the sea some ten million years ago. At one time, they may have stood almost two kilometres high, but both volcanoes blew their tops some five hundred thousand years ago and the remnants currently poke up about half that height.

As we wind along the highway leading to the Banks Peninsula, I can't help but wonder why, with all this natural mayhem about, there isn't more theological placating going on. The patron saint of New Zealand is Francis Xavier, the seventeenth-century Jesuit who spent several years bare-footing about in the general neighbourhood. In addition to converting heathens, St. Francis had a nice little sideline calming storms, which must have appealed to early navigators, but even so, there's not a single burg named in his honour. In fact, a brief glance at the map shows there's damned little in the way of hagiography anywhere in the country. There is a resort town near Nelson called St. Arnaud, but it's named for the Marshall of France who fought beside the English in the Crimean War in 1854—not for the thirteenth-century inquisitor who got an early pass to paradise for sticking his nose too far into the business of Albigensian heretics. Christchurch is a good start, but considering all the volcanoes about, wouldn't a town called Holy Smokes be more appropriate?

The highway begins to climb through wooded valleys, until it reaches higher ground where vineyards and orchards compete for sun. We round a bend, and below us, Akaroa Harbour comes into view. Vistas like this remind one that it is great to be alive— the ancient crater of the volcano has burst into the sea and is now a magnificent string of blue water, garlanded on both sides by emerald green pastureland. The port town is a line of painted wooden houses and warehouses, stretching along the dock like a set of brightly coloured children's blocks. Shafts of sunlight cut through the overhead cloud and dance across the harbour, weaving their way through the yachts and fishing trawlers that bob at anchor offshore.

We stop at a French café, bordering the sea. I order a strawberry crepe with whipped crème, while Linda opts for the chocolate variety. Although neither goes particularly well with our wine, that's okay—the dolphins that occasionally break water and splash about are more than enough distraction. Unfortunately, Akaroa's delights are dampened by the arrival of a squall and, reluctantly, we return to Christchurch.

Our intention is to explore farther down the coast over the next few days, but the weather continues to crap all over our plans. Worse, the heaviest rain moves up the coast, threatening to cut off our retreat to the North Island. We reluctantly realize that winter has come early to New Zealand, and our only recourse is to move on and forgo the return trip to Auckland. Fortunately, A2Z Rental Cars has a local outlet in Christchurch. We check with our airline; there is room for two on the next flight out. We sell our ghetto blaster and pasta pot to Les and turn in the Egg.

As we sit in the airport waiting for our flight, I cast back over our sojourn in New Zealand. In six weeks, we travelled almost ten thousand kilometres, from the subtropical suburbs of Auckland to the frosty heights of the South Alps. We never found a place as enjoyable as Manly, but that might simply be due to our own rush to see as much as possible. Who knows, after all, if we will ever pass this way again?

I think about the happy people we met—our Queenstown waitress Sabrina, the children fishing on the beach in Nelson—but also about those unhappy with their lives—Sue and Phil's resentment of the tall-poppy syndrome. But, come to think of it, if most parts of Canada could, at any moment, do a deadly version of the boogaloo or blow up with the force of a thousand atomic bombs, I might be a tad surly myself.

They call our flight, and we join the queue to board. I peer out through the airport terminal window for one last look at New Zealand, but the mist and fog limit my view. I silently thank all the Kiwis who made our visit so enjoyable and apologize to the not inconsiderable number of hotel managers for leaving dirty dishes in the sink.

It is time to hit our final destination: Fiji. ■

CHAPTER 12

Palapa Hammock
and Lie Down

O ur race with Mother Nature goes international. With impeccable timing, we arrive in Fiji, on the main island of Viti Levu, the day before a cyclone. As we step off the plane, the terminal is awash with tourists in sarongs and flip-flops trying desperately to get on the last available flights out before the airport shuts down. Already, rain is beginning to fall, and gusts of wind are twisting the palm trees about like skinny hula dancers. We hail a taxi out front and climb in. We ask our cab driver, a Fijian man in a tropical shirt, where we should go.

"Check into the Viti Lodge," he suggests. "It's built from cement."

The lodge is a few kilometres from the airport, along the road leading into the town of Nadi. As promised, the three-storey building, shaped in a curve, looks solidly built. The desk clerk is more than happy to offer us a room; most of his clientele have already fled. "And it's not even going to hit us directly," he sniffs.

The room is decorated in Holiday Inn chic—beige walls, teal carpet, and a smattering of what I like to call prison art, bucolic, semi-abstract country landscapes painted by someone long deprived of the outside world. I am a little concerned about the glass doors leading out onto the patio, but the bellhop tells us that they are specially constructed to be unbreakable. I can't help but recall that the *Titanic* was specially constructed to be unsinkable, but keep my thoughts to myself.

The hotel restaurant is closed, and so we make do with some snacks from a dispensing machine at the end of the hall. We settle into our room, and as the winds pick up in fury and pound the hotel in noisy gusts, we sit in front of the TV, eating spicy corn chips, sipping diet soda, and watching the news. Canada gets a mention—we watch a French starlet decorously fling herself across a baby seal, vowing that she is willing to be clubbed in order to protect it. Thankfully, the power fails and the TV goes out, but the windows hold.

By the next morning, the skies are clear. The power, however, is still out. Without air conditioning, the room becomes hot and clammy, and Linda and I decide that we might as well go for a jog and sweat outside, as opposed to sweating inside. We don running gear and head down to the reception area, where the clerk recommends we cross the main highway and take a side road toward the coast.

The island nation of Fiji sits about fourteen hundred kilometres north of New Zealand, fifteen degrees south of the equator. It consists of more than three hundred islands, spread out over a pie-shaped area some four hundred kilometres across. The two biggest islands, Vanua Levu and Viti Levu, are remnants of continental land masses that broke off and staggered like drunken sailors into the middle of the ocean several million years ago and never made it back. Somehow or other, explorers from New Guinea managed to find the islands about thirty-five hundred years ago, but the majority of native Fijians are related to Melanesians, whose migration here began around AD 100. Ethnic Indians, the second major group on the islands, are largely descended from the Hindus who were indentured by the British in the nineteenth century to work on their plantations. Today, the eight hundred thousand-odd inhabitants are a mix of native Melanesians, ethnic Indians, and Europeans.

The most popular local pastime is the imbibing of *yaqona*, a mildly intoxicating brown soup, traditionally made from kava roots chewed by virgins. Another fun national sport is the military coup, practised by the native Fijians whenever the ethnic Indians get too rambunctious in Parliament. When not getting stoned or chasing each other with bayonets, they generally settle down and muddle along in typical South Pacific fashion. The leading sectors of the economy are tourism, tropical fruits, and sugar.

That explains why Linda and I are currently running through what seems to be mile after mile of sugar cane. The sweet smell of the bamboo-like plant has mixed with the dampness of the cyclone's rain to create a thick, cloying atmosphere, which vaguely reminds me of hot maple syrup. There isn't a hint of a breeze, and the tropical sun beating down on us makes me wish I was wearing a hat. Over the last month or so, our jogging gait has levelled off at around eight kilometres an hour, fast enough to get a good cardiovascular workout, but slow enough to avoid extensive damage if, by happenstance, one's attention wanders sufficiently to stumble into a tent guy wire. We run for about half an hour, but there is still no sign of the coast and, reluctantly, we turn and head back. As we retrace our steps, the air becomes hotter and hotter. There is no traffic along the road, and except for the occasional cane toad that hops out of the wet ditch and scampers across the blistering tarmac, we are completely alone.

As we trudge along, I note a thick column of greyish black smoke twisting lazily upward in the distance, somewhere toward the mythical shore. It reminds me of a similar column of smoke I saw years ago in Thailand, when the body of a Vietnamese boat refugee washed onto the shore of the island of Koh Samui, and the locals cremated it. I can't decide if this funeral pyre is Buddhist, Baptist, or Hindu.

My head begins to ache and I realize that I might be getting a little too much sun. Belatedly, I conclude that we are in danger of being overexposed to the heat and humidity. We press on until we arrive back at Viti Lodge, where, mercifully, the air conditioning has been restored, and we are able to cool down sufficiently to avoid heat stroke. I stand in the shower, hoping that the cold water will erase the feeling of malaise that grips me. Is it just the heat and the bad weather, or is it the thought of returning home? I'm going to have to take up a sport less depressing than running—perhaps chasing French starlets around ice flows.

The next morning, all effects of heat stroke have passed and Linda and I are both feeling much better. The hotel's interior decorations linger on, however, providing sufficient threat of nausea to prompt us to seek more amenable lodging.

Taking a taxi, we head off in the direction of what my island map promisingly describes as Mudflat Beach. Thomas, our cab driver, is a genial native Fijian, eminently suited to his job, since he is about five feet tall and weighs some three hundred pounds and rarely bounces off the ceiling when we hit a pothole. After another tour of cane fields along a paved road, we come to a turnoff and bounce down a muddy track, until we finally reach the coast.

As its name suggests, Mudflat Beach is not the most enticing destination. The shoreline is marked for several kilometres by a mix of coral sand and black silt, and the odour of kelp and biomanure wafts through the taxi's window. Our cabbie insists that it all looks much nicer at high tide, and besides, his uncle runs a resort just down the road that is one of the island's finest places. Admiring his unbiased opinion, we agree to check it out.

Mudflat Resort is carved out of a level spot on the sand dunes that back onto the beach; the dune grass is kept cropped by a pair of ancient horses tethered to a palm tree. The core of the resort is a large restaurant/hangout, essentially a thatched-roof *palapa*, exposed to the elements via the simple technique of not having walls. The laughter of several guests from within it mixes with the sound of Eric Clapton unplugged. It has the general unkempt air of a Sunday morning after a big Saturday night blowout, and we take an instant liking to it.

Uncle Ratu is the spitting image of Thomas, only with grey, curly hair. He escorts us along a string of cabanas, until he finds an empty one. Like the restaurant/hangout, the cabin is up on stilts and sports a thatched roof, but it also has walls, windows, and a door—minor but essential touches that I feel really make a difference. Inside, the floor is covered with highly polished wood and the furniture is made of teak. We agree on the spot to a week's stay.

Life at the Mudflat Resort alternates between desultory and semi-comatose. The desultory part consists of finding a hammock and lounging in the shade of palm trees, while reading a book; the semi-comatose portion is dedicated to the *yaqona* ceremony. We are sitting on our cabana porch admiring the sunset over the Pacific when, precisely at sundown, Uncle Ratu appears in the restaurant with a large bowl of brown fluid. Although I spot precious few candidates for virginity in the vicinity, I conclude this must be kava. We join Ratu there, along with several other guests. After dipping into the fluid with a small bowl, he offers everyone gathered around a sample. I take a healthy sip—it is peppery and somewhat starchy, but not unpleasant, and my fingers tingle and a mild buzz sets in. I find myself relaxing and enjoying the strumming of the guitar as one of Ratu's family sings a traditional song.

Before we lapse into a total stupor, however, Ratu's wife, Jasmine, announces that the evening's meal is ready. She has baked whitefish in a mix of lemon, garlic, soy sauce, and ginger, which she serves with baked yams, coconut rice, and a fruit salad of mangoes, pineapples, oranges, papaya, and banana. We wash it all down with local beer, and then stagger off to our cabana to retire for the evening, lulled to sleep by the sound of the incoming surf.

The next morning, Linda and I arise early and head out for a run on the beach before the heat of the day has a chance to build. When most people think of tropical beaches, they likely picture white, sugary sand, clear blue skies dotted with fluffy clouds, and palm trees swaying gently in the wind. They obviously haven't seen the postcards from around here. In addition to greyish sand, Mudflat Beach features a pleasant assortment of iron pipe drains, plastic six-pack holders, and what appears to be a rusty beached whale. It is, in fact, an eighteen-metre-long, inter-island ferry, which was pushed ashore by the cyclone. The local villagers, brawny-armed Indian lads, are climbing over the tilting hull and energetically helping themselves to the fixtures, in an improvised bit of salvaging that would do a crew of Barbary pirates proud.

We skirt around a big pile of brass fittings and shiny white urinals and continue on our way past a long row of cane that abuts the beach. We come to a clearing where a pile of black stumps marks the remnants of the funeral pyre we spotted yesterday. The embers are still smoking, but that doesn't deter the pack of wild dogs that are listlessly scavenging through the ash.

We are heading back toward the resort when Linda first notices the sand fleas. In my personal experience, being in the great outdoors with a natural blonde is a wonderful experience—virtually every critter that likes blood goes for them first. As I run nonchalantly along, I spot Linda swatting at her legs. I look down and realize the sand is almost completely covered with tiny black mites, leaping up and down in evident glee at the thought of fresh blood. We detour toward the surf, hoping that the salty water deters them, but the dirty little beggars don snorkels and pursue us relentlessly and don't give up the chase until we are almost back to the resort. By the time we reach the safety of our cabin, Linda's legs are covered in angry red welts.

"You're going to need to put cream on those," says Jasmine, when she sees the bites. "The closest pharmacy is in town."

The commuter service to Nadi consists of a flatbed Toyota truck, to which the enterprising owner has bolted some wooden benches. The return fare, which is the local equivalent of fifty cents, does not even begin to cover the insurance risk. We cling to the steel posts supporting the aluminum roof shade, as we jostle along the resort's access road to the main highway, where we pick up three more passengers and several chickens. The birds ride free.

If Stalin had ever set out to design a tropical village, I suspect it would look exactly like Nadi. As we reach the outskirts of town, we pass block after block of post-and-slab concrete housing, each building given its own unique charm by the addition of a wide assortment of personal objects piled onto balconies, including goats. Our truck stops at the main market, a two-storey facility crammed with stalls selling everything from remote-control toy robots to kava root. The shoppers, virtually all of them ethnic Indian women, lug large cellulose sacks on their heads. When we enter the interior, we are immediately overwhelmed by the smell of freshly ground spices: cumin, pepper, and clove. A helpful shopkeeper directs us to the pharmacy, where the proprietor, a very accommodating chap in his late eighties, offers to sell us not only sand-flea cream, but an enticing array of other "stimulating" medications.

We decline the latter and continue our exploration of the market. Specifically, I am searching for a souvenir, but not the usual taxidermal blowfish sort of memento, mind you. I'm thinking of something a little more interesting. Centuries ago, native Fijians were well known for their taste for *bakolo*, or human flesh. Various tribes waged war with one another, and the victors carted their victims back home for an extensive feast. Numerous missionaries recorded that limbs and entrails would be wrapped in banana leaves and cooked in special ovens until tender. Although the practice died out with the cessation of tribal warfare in the nineteenth century, I am told you can still buy the accompanying Cannibal Chutney. I stop at a booth full of various canned goods and inquire.

"Sorry, we do not have that," explains the vendor. "But I do have a special fork that was used to eat the brains." He holds up a thin, wooden utensil. "It makes a nifty gift."

Now, I haven't used "nifty" as a guide to purchasing since I was about twelve. I used to think, for instance, it would be nifty to own a walking cane with a sword hidden in it or a flamethrower that would tuck inconspicuously into my backpack. Since puberty, however, I have generally opted in favour of practical and economical. Mind you, the fork *is* nifty, but I had my heart set on the chutney and take a pass.

Linda and I are about to leave the market when we stumble on what passes for the food court, a series of tiny lunch counters surrounded by stools, upon which you belly up to the grub. We sit down at one and a cheerful, chubby woman, wearing an orange and purple sari, ladles out two bowls of vegetable curry. Although we were warned to watch out for dodgy food in the marketplace, it smells too good to pass up. Besides, what harm can a few vegetables do? It is hot and creamy, with spicy coconut sauce, and goes very well with the garlic naan, made fresh in a clay oven on the premises. For the equivalent of a dollar, we both have two helpings.

Satisfyingly full, we exit the market and find our truck driver, who has stocked up on beer and rice for the resort. We are halfway to Mudflat Beach when the first rumblings in my digestive tract signal that all is not well. I glance at Linda, who is experiencing similar gastronomic distress. Fortunately, the driver is in a hurry to finish the day's run, and we make it to the resort with minutes to spare before our meal decides to evacuate.

It *was* brilliant curry, though.

We bump into Thomas the taxi driver the next day, when he drops someone off at the resort. Perhaps I'm feeling a bit peevish due to last night's curry laxative, but I confess to Thomas that, so far, I am less than smitten with the charms of Fiji.

"Why are you lazing about here?" he demands. "You should take a cruise out to see the Mamanucas—that's where you see the best of Fiji."

The Mamanucas are a string of coral islands that run in an arc north and west of Nadi, and it just so happens that Thomas has another uncle who runs a tour boat out every day. The boat in question is a two-masted schooner, over thirty-six-metres long and made of teak. I agree that this would be a wonderful tonic, and Linda and I set out from port that afternoon, accompanied by thirty or so fellow travellers, an eclectic flotsam of Australians, Kiwis, Americans, Canadians, and a Swede. One nice thing about being on the road for a year is that you tend to bump into people you've seen thousands of kilometres away. In this case, the Swede happens to be Sven, the same biker we met in the Banana Bar in Rarotonga.

I can't believe that only seven months have passed since we landed in the Cook Islands. I reintroduce myself to Sven, who is wearing a sleeveless T-shirt to highlight his tattoos, and he shows me a real beauty of a devil he had done in Bangkok, which winks at me as he rolls his biceps. I also vaguely recognize two of the Kiwis from the gay pride parade in Auckland, but it's a bit difficult to tell without the tutus and I don't get a chance to talk to them, as they are busily chatting up the crew, three Fijian lads. The crewmen are far more interested in preparing a bowl of *yaqona* than romance, however. Sitting at the base of the foremast, they whip up a batch of kava and generously offer it to everyone, including several children under ten. One horrified mother from San Diego snatches her boy away. "He's on Ritalin," she explains to us.

Although the windward breeze is sufficiently brisk to make good time, the crew becomes involved in a kava-drinking contest with two Australians in Billabong T-shirts, which is never a good idea, and the sails remain furled as we motor to our destination via diesel. After about an hour scuttling over the open seas, we arrive at a large reef that circles a lagoon and an island. The captain drops anchor outside the reef, and we take an inflatable tender boat through a gap in the coral and land upon the beach. As promised by Thomas, the island is a tropical paradise, with a long, sandy beach of crushed white coral, swaying coconut trees, and a turquoise lagoon—just like the postcards.

Linda and I wander over to the resort restaurant, where the menu, all in U.S. dollars, states that a glass of Coke costs five bucks. We opt instead for a stroll along the beach, passing a resort hut where a woman and her two children are relaxing with paperback books on the front porch.

"We love it *heah*," she exclaims, in a nasal Boston accent that would nicely stand in for a foghorn in an emergency. We are tempted to pack our bags and join her for a few days until we inquire about the nightly charge. "Three hundred *dallahs*," she notes.

At first, I can't believe my ears—this is about ten times what we are paying at our resort, and the cabins are essentially the same, only the beach differs. "Is that Fiji money?" I ask.

The woman purses her lips and knits her brows in a quizzical manner—I get the distinct impression that, until now, it hasn't occurred to her that Fiji has its own currency.

Just then, Sven walks by with a pair of Heinekens in each hand. Ms. Boston silently watches him recede down the beach, leans toward us, as if this is going to limit the rust-removing abilities of her voice, and says, "But it's worth it to get away from all the riff-raff, you know?" We solemnly agree and then head back to the boat to rejoin our group of reprobates; maybe the Ozzies have left some kava.

If we can't rent paradise, at least we can buy an entrance ticket. The next day, we decide to head for the Garden of the Sleeping Giant, which was established in 1977 by none other than Raymond Burr, of *Perry Mason* fame. Although Burr was a well-known screen actor for many years prior to his TV success (one of his best roles is the creepy neighbour who kills his wife and stuffs her in a trunk in Hitchcock's *Rear Window*), the money he made from acting as a gruff attorney and his subsequent hitch as a gruff police chief on *Ironside* was sufficient to bankroll anything his heart desired.

After *Ironside* ended in 1975, he and his partner started a plantation on Fiji to hybridize orchids, a mutual passion. Over the course of several decades, they were responsible for the addition of some fifteen hundred new hybrids to the international catalogue.

After Burr died in 1993, the plantation evolved into a tourist attraction. The garden itself sits a few kilometres inland from the sea, nestled in a valley carved into the side of a range of forest-covered hills. The hills act as a rain catch, squeezing the necessary moisture from the clouds that roll overhead. As the garden's name implies, the hills in the area resemble a huge reclining giant, and the garden is near his left armpit.

We take the local bus from our resort to the entrance. A series of wooden walkways leads us past a lily pond and up to the various orchid beds. You gotta love orchids. Some thirty thousand specimens and another hundred thousand hybrids have been catalogued over the years on every continent save Antarctica. They range in size from microscopic to more than six metres in width, and many live on air, their roots gathering moisture and nourishment when it rains. There are orchids that are shaped like lady-bumblebee bums to attract horny males, orchids that give off a putrefying stink to attract dung flies, and an underground orchid in Australia that pollinates itself using ants. Charles Darwin loved orchids and used their odd, adaptive shapes to help formulate his theory of evolution. In fact, he got the raspberry from his peers when he described an orchid that exploded to distribute its pollen. Orchids are a real pain to cultivate, though, and only the most lunatic of gardeners choose them. Personally, I've had greater success with mould.

Burr was mostly enamoured with their great beauty, a combination of colour, delicacy, and symmetry. As we march up and down the walkways, we gaze at a rainbow of flowers, from mustard yellow to creamy white and deep, red fuchsia. Eventually, Linda and I come to a bungalow, which was Burr's home when he visited Fiji. Still furnished with his belongings, the dining table is set for afternoon tea and a walking cane rests against his rocking chair. I can picture him sitting there, late in his life, clutching a cup of oolong tea and admiring the fruit of his labour, with only the occasional exploding orchid to disturb the zen-like tranquility. After he died, his body was cremated in traditional Baptist fashion and the ashes scattered over, you guessed it, New Westminster, British Columbia. I told you orchid guys are crazy.

It is our last day on Fiji. Even though we've only been here a week, we have to cut our stay short. Our funds are severely depleted. Tomorrow, Linda and I fly back to Canada to once again insert ourselves into the inertia of North American life— SUVs, McDonald's, reality TV—but right now we are sitting on our cabin porch, waiting for the sun to set. We talk about all the people we have met and the things we have seen, as if by doing so, we will fix them more firmly in our hearts.

"I wonder if Porkchop ever went to second base with Violet?" asks Linda.

"I suspect he went to the emergency ward first," I reply.

"When I turn eighty, I want to have a pair of red-leather, high-heeled sandals, just like Gertrude," says Linda.

"When I turn eighty, I want a case of red wine from the Hunter Valley. And I want to sit on Manly Beach and drink it."

"Remember the silly little bird at Pancake Rocks?"

"I can still smell the salt spray of the ocean."

"That's because you're sitting beside one, silly."

"Oh, yeah."

We fall silent as the sun dips into the ocean—immense, magenta, wavering—then disappears. "Do you regret coming on this trip?"

Linda reaches over and hugs me. "Not for a second."

"Are you happy?"

"Yes, I am."

"Even if we didn't get to stay in Manly?"

"It was wonderful just going there with you, and everywhere else, too. How about you? Are you happy?"

I don't know. I thought I had found happiness in Rarotonga, an island as close to paradise as you can get. There, everyone takes care of everyone else and there's no hunger, or lack of clothing, or need for shelter. But nobody owns anything, and there's no reward for trying harder. Above all, there was nothing to *do*. In Australia, the land of plenty, everyone works to play. They have great respect for the individual, but they feel that anyone who gets ahead had to cheat to do it. In New Zealand, I always felt very comfortable and welcome and safe—except for the ghost, the wrong-way drivers, and the earthquakes, of course. And while the Fijian people are friendly and accommodating, there are too many coups whenever the native Fijians begin to worry that the Indian population is getting too uppity.

I wasn't particularly surprised by my ambivalence. We met lots of people who have lived in the South Pacific far longer than us, and they didn't know either. Des and Tabita were unhappy because there was no future for their child; Chops was unhappy because he had no one to love. Folks in Oz were unhappy because beer was so expensive, and Kiwis didn't like their own penchant for cutting down those who got too far above the rest—the tall-poppy syndrome. The only ones we met who were truly joyful were kids; maybe happiness is just something that adults don't deserve.

A sliver of silvery moon hangs heavily over now-invisible Mudflat Beach. I want the evening to stop and everything to stay as it is, now and forever. But, despite my best efforts, the southern stars slowly dip into the ocean, one by one, and disappear. Soon it will be time to leave, and our journey will be over.

Uncle Ratu comes along with his bowl, now empty. I wave to him, and he alters course to join us on the veranda. "Uncle Ratu, are you happy?"

Ratu's face breaks out in a big smile. "Yes, I am happy."

"Why is that? Because you have a successful business?"

"My business is doing well, but no, that is not why."

"You live in a gorgeous part of the world?"

"Fiji is indeed beautiful, but no, that is not why."

"You have a large and healthy family?"

"That is very important, but it is only part of the reason."

"Tell me, then."

Uncle Ratu scratches his chin for a moment, thinking. "All material wealth is fleeting, and nowhere is perfect. As for the people we love, everyone passes on someday."

"That doesn't sound much like happiness to me."

"That's because happiness isn't a thing, or a place, or person."

"What is it then?"

"It is a state of mind. If you want to find happiness, look for it in your heart." Uncle Ratu gathers up his bowl and turns toward home. He waves to us and disappears into the night, but his parting words hang in the warm, tropical air.

"Nothing is ever going to work out exactly as you wish it. You can only enjoy the moment." ■

Epilogue

Surprisingly, it wasn't all that difficult returning to Calgary and settling in after almost a year away. Through good fortune and perseverance, we were able to establish our own careers; Linda served as an IT systems consultant and I wrote feature stories for magazines and newspapers. Instead of buying a home, we rented a magical bungalow near the river, which was just as well, as we were soon off on further adventures. Thanks largely to Linda's work, we lived in Paris and London and travelled to many parts of the world.

And we are very happy. This is partly because we work for ourselves and we don't worry about having the biggest home or the fanciest car. But, mostly, it is because we have learned that no matter where you go, happiness is in your heart.

It has been more than a decade since our journey to the South Pacific. Fred the rooster, who woke us up every morning at the Paradise Inn in Rarotonga, has long since gone to that big stew pot in the sky. Porkchop, I suspect, has forsaken his career cooking airline food to be the public health minister, while Violet has found her true love and is the proud mother of a large family.

Our kindly Australian neighbour Gertrude, bless her soul, is long gone, but I suspect Lucky Luke is still energetically placing unsuspecting car renters at risk. Over in New Zealand, Les is probably still vacuuming shag rug to the beat of our ghetto blaster, while wise Uncle Ratu is mixing kava and enjoying the Fijian sunsets.

As for my mate Greg, his dream finally came through. The next time you're in Manly, stop by *Scoozame* and order an espresso. Give him our love, and tell him we'll be back again soon. I promise.

And even though *Magnus the Magnificent*, the book I wrote in Australia, has been read and rejected by dozens of publishers, it hasn't stopped me from writing. But then, it's the journey, not the destination, isn't it?

One last thing; in the prologue, I wondered if we deserve happiness. The answer is yes—each and every one of us. And it's yours for the asking. Just remember to try and put back more than you take. ▪

Acknowledgements

I wish to thank the people of the Cook Islands, Australia, New Zealand, and Fiji for greeting us with open arms and warm hearts. I am also indebted to a wide spectrum of sources that helped me flesh out many of the geographical details and lore of the places we visited, including *Lonely Planet Rarotonga and the Cook Islands* by Tony Wheeler and Nancy Keller (Lonely Planet, 1995), the New Zealand Automobile Association, and Wikipedia.

I also wish to thank Alex Frazer-Harrison and Geri Rowlatt for editing the manuscript, David Drummond for designing the cover and Dean Pickup for designing the interior, Meaghan Craven for shepherding the book through to completion, and Charlene Dobmeier for offering me the opportunity to tell this tale. ■